John Pritchard is Bishop of Jarrow. He was Archdeacon of Canterbury and, before that, Warden of Cranmer Hall, Durham. He has served in parishes in Birmingham and Taunton and has been Diocesan Youth Officer for Bath and Wells diocese. Other books by the author include *The Intercessions Handbook, Living the Gospel Stories Today, How to Pray* and *Leading Intercessions*. He is married with two daughters.

Beginning Again

For those who want to begin, or begin again,
on the Christian Journey

John Pritchard

For Wendy, Amanda and Nicola
loving companions on the journey

Published in Great Britain in 2000

Society for Promoting Christian Knowledge
36 Causton Street
London SW1P 4ST

Illustrations by Paul Judson

British Library Cataloguing-in-Publication Data
A catalogue record for this book is available from the British Library

ISBN 0–281–05265–4

10 9 8 7 6 5 4 3 2

Typeset by Deltatype Ltd, Birkenhead, Wirral

Printed in Great Britain by Ashford Colour Press

Contents

Introduction

This book is written for people who want to be on a journey – specifically the Christian journey. It is written for people who believe they could be on to something really important, but are not sure how to get going. It is written for people on the edge of the Christian faith, just inside or just outside.

It is also written for Christians who are in need of beginning again on the Christian journey:

✳ evangelicals who have lost their first love of Christ

✳ catholics who have got over-familiar with the sacraments

✳ 'Spirit-filled' Christians who have begun to leak.

In fact it is probably for more people than we might suspect.

I often meet people who want some practical help in taking the Christian journey seriously but who can only find strait-jackets to try on – one particular way of praying or reading the Bible for instance. It is my belief that God has given us a huge variety of ways of making the Christian journey, and we should be using a whole range of approaches. It sometimes seems that we are holding on to a closed box with one lonely stone rolling around inside instead of exploring the treasure trove available to us, full of precious stones inviting our enjoyment.

The further I go in the Christian journey the more it seems that I have only just put a toe into the ocean. As we stand before the immensity of that ocean (which is God), we do not want to be told that there is only one swimming costume to wear and only one way of swimming. We want to get out there and enjoy the freedom, the exhilaration and the challenge of the swim.

This is unashamedly a 'how to' book. There are, for example, lorry-loads of books on prayer: indeed my own shelves groan with them. I want to encourage people not to read more about prayer, but to *pray*. Similarly, not to read *about* the Bible but to get to grips with it themselves, and not to moan about the church but to enjoy it. I hope that for some people, this book will do just that and help them discover more of the riches of Christ.

1 Starting and re-starting with God

Many of us . . .

* want to take faith more seriously but don't want to become too religious

* like the look of Jesus but get a bit anxious about the Church

* know that our faith has run into the sand

* occasionally get mildly drunk on beauty

* don't like to admit we have spiritual longings

* want to live life up to the brim – plus a bit

* reckon we haven't done too well in trying to be a Christian

* once experienced faith as dynamic, but now seem to have lost the plot

* find it difficult to pray and read the Bible but still feel they could be really important

* sometimes find a deep longing welling up inside us

* don't want to be kidnapped by religious Thought Police

* get frustrated by religious jargon

* want to experience something real in all this God-talk

* dislike one-word answers to spiritual questions

* don't want to be guilty of self-deception

* would love to entrust our lives to the wild wonder of a great God

* once met someone we might call holy – and it was electric!

* know our need of God

✻ are fascinated by Jesus

✻ would like more of the Spirit.

If you can say 'yes' to many of those statements you may well be looking for a way of starting or starting again on the serious (but not solemn) business of knowing God or being a Christian. A Christian of course is not primarily someone who tries hard, goes to church or believes six impossible things before breakfast. A Christian is someone who has put his or her life together, in a relationship of trust, with Jesus Christ. The New Testament does not have a single image of this. It plays with different images: knowing Christ (Philippians 3.10), receiving Christ (Revelation 3.20), coming to Christ (John 6.37), Christ living in the believer (Galatians 2.20). The important point is not the precise description but the coming together, in relationship, of Christ and the individual.

It is worth trying out a number of images now in order to explore more clearly what this might mean for us and where we've got to in our spiritual journey. I want to offer more than one image because, as I hope to make clear in the rest of the book, different approaches help different people. The four images I offer here are these:

1 **The mountain.**
2 **The bowl.**
3 **The border.**
4 **The journey.**

Once we have understood a little more clearly where we are in terms of our faith, and where we might have got stuck, we can then look at how to get moving again with fresh ways of approaching prayer, the Bible, belonging to the church, and Christian lifestyle. That's what this book is all about.

The mountain

> **Exercise:**
>
> ✻ Look at Figure 1 and imagine that the mountain represents God, Christ, the Christian faith – whichever you find easiest to work with.
>
> ✻ Now think about which of those figures on the mountain represents you in your relationship with God etc. Are you like the

Figure 1

figure hanging on grimly, or sheltering in a cave, or climbing happily, or what?

✳ Now explore in your mind why you are most like that figure. What are the aspects of your experience which make that the most accurate representation of where you are?

✳ Now think about which figure most closely represented you, say, five or ten years ago. And what was going on then to make that the case?

✳ Now think about which figure you would like to be in two years time. Would you like to be resting happily half way up, helping others on the climb, swinging charismatically, or what? How serious are you in that intent? And what might you do to get there?

Remember, there is no value-judgement in your choice here. This is entirely an exercise in self-understanding. But knowing where you have come from and where you are now can help you make choices about your faith journey. The old philosopher's tag remains true: 'Know yourself.'

The bowl

Imagine a medium-sized bowl of water and a nearby sponge. The bowl of water represents God, Christ, the Christian faith, the church – again, whichever image you find most helpful. The sponge represents us. Now think of a number of options. None of them are supposed to have a value-judgement attached to them. They are simply descriptive aids to help us locate ourselves in relation to faith and the church.

1 **The sponge remains quite separate from the bowl.** Some people keep at a safe distance from the bowl. Either they don't believe the water is drinkable, or they don't believe it has anything that is relevant to their experience and needs.

2 **The sponge is close to the bowl, but outside the rim, and static.** Some people don't mind being close to the church or the faith and will gladly help their partner to decorate the church or deliver leaflets, but they don't want to get involved in the water itself. Perhaps they got wet once and were badly let down. They want to stay dry. There is no journey to be made.

3 **The sponge makes occasional sorties into the water.** Many people want the faith to be there for them, usually in the form of the church, at special times. Christmas is a favourite, but so too are weddings, baptisms and funerals. Easter is a possibility, or Mother's Day, and in some places, harvest. It's good and reassuring to have the church there and its services are appreciated. Sometimes, indeed, the sponge does actually respond to the water – it feels good. But the truth is that life is very busy and the sponge would get clogged up by too much water.

4 **The sponge is inside the bowl and rests half in and half out of the water.** Many people come to church regularly and enjoy the life and worship of the community. They are fed and watered by the faith but retain a certain ambivalence about the water itself. Those who dive in completely often seem to become obsessive and to have no other life except the church. In any case there are a number of ways in which the faith is still not fully convincing or real in experience. The bowl and the water are fine – as far as they go.

5 **The sponge is immersed in the water.** Some people inch their way, or dive(!), right into the water. They want to be soaked in the Spirit of Christ so that they are in him and he is in them. 'If anyone is *in* Christ there is a new creation' (2 Corinthians 5.17). This is the life of surrender to Christ. This doesn't mean that we have 'arrived'. This is just the start, and we will fail again and again. There are other dangers too – of becoming addicted to the life of the bowl, for example! The point of the sponge being filled with 'living water' (John 4.10) is that we can then go and share the water outside the bowl and in the world.

The question is 'where am I as a "sponge" in relation to the water? If none of the images above precisely fits my position, then what variation would be more accurate?' If the image helps, use it; if not, try another.

The border

Imagine a border between two countries. The border-line wanders through the countryside, sometimes clearly marked by a border post on a road or a fence going through the fields, but sometimes quite lost on the hillsides and the marshes. The border is a metaphor for the line between two other countries – the kingdom of God and the kingdom of self. In the latter, we are

7

in control, making the rules, issuing the currency, shaping the culture; in the former, God is in control of the 'heartland' and everything flows from his 'just and gentle rule'.

How then do we pass from one country to the other?

Some people wander across the border without even really noticing they have done so. Yes, there was a little sign they passed, or a wooden gate they went through, but nothing very much. After a while, however, they begin to notice that the countryside is looking different – richer and healthier – and the people are speaking a more poetic and gracious language. In a similar way, probably the majority of people wander into the kingdom of God without being very conscious of it. They have been attracted by some of the things they have heard about life in the other country and they have simply set off towards it some time ago. Yes, there were some markers at an important stretch of the journey, but by and large it was a natural movement across the border.

Others find the crossing rather more decisive. They come up to a border checkpoint and there they have to decide if they really want to cross over or not. No one is stopping them; it is simply that they want to be sure it is a reasonable and right thing to do. Again, a number of people become active Christians by travelling up to the border gradually and then thoughtfully counting the cost. Then they decide that they want to make a commitment to Christ and his kingdom, and they enter 'the promised land'.

Others again make a rather more dramatic entrance. When they get to the border there are guards determined to stop their escape into the kingdom of light. The would-be Christian therefore makes a break for it, and crosses the border with all guns blazing, under a hail of fire, and collapses panting but victorious on the far side. He or she, of course, is the Christian who is most likely to write a book about the experience! And these books tend to make ordinary Christians who entered the kingdom by a less dramatic method, feel rather inferior – even to doubt whether they are properly in the kingdom at all.

We need to recognize that the first two methods of entry are by far the most common. Indeed one piece of careful research showed that around 70 per cent of Christians regarded their coming to faith as gradual. And of the other 30 per cent most would probably have made careful decisions rather than dramatic breakthroughs.

What matters therefore is not the method of entry but the fact that we are there.

The journey

Perhaps the most helpful image to help us understand where we are in relation to God, and the Christian faith therefore, is the *journey*. Here is a common denominator, an experience with which most people can identify. A journey has:

* a starting-point

* different episodes, involving pleasures and crises, achievements and disasters

* a sense of arrival at significant places

* periods in the wilderness, and areas marked 'there be dragons'

* special companions and group experiences.

In particular this approach allows us to see the interrelationship of our Christian journey with other important events in our lives. In a faith where God gets thoroughly involved in the whole fabric of human life, you would expect some interaction between the spiritual, physical and emotional dimensions of our lives. Bereavement, for example, can bring about the birth or death of faith, as can marriage, parenthood, or leaving home. Problems in health or marriage can profoundly affect the journey, as can meeting a particular person, be it a dynamic curate or a future wife.

Another way of saying this comes from Paul: 'We know that in all things God works for good with those who love him.' (Romans 8.28) God is never inactive, a passive observer, but always the active agent of change, seeking constantly to draw people into his love.

Exercise

* Use Figure 2 which shows a path running from the top right to the bottom left. See this as your faith journey and mark on the path the significant events, experiences, people, crises etc. which have affected your journey. Go right back to your earliest memories. These events and experiences will be both human and divine because the two are inextricably linked.

* It may be that your journey is a very recent one and you can't see much having happened in the past by way of a spiritual journey. That may be entirely accurate, but do also look more searchingly through some of the significant moments of your

human journey; it may be that in retrospect you now see a touch of the divine hand, which you would not have recognized as that in the past.

* Try as far as possible to do without words, which we so often hide behind, and instead use symbols, pictures and images to tell the story.

* Take a while over this and try to be very honest in seeing how and why certain events moved you on – or back – in your faith journey.

* It can be particularly valuable to do this with others and in pairs or threes to share some of the significant moments on the journey – always remembering that you are in charge of how much you want to say.

Having reached this point on the journey, how do you want it to develop?

We need to remember here that all sorts of things will affect how free we are to choose our way ahead. Our life circumstances at the moment will be particularly important. A young mother without a second to call her own, an executive travelling all over the world, and a widow struggling to remake her life, will all have different constraints and opportunities in their Christian journey. Other factors may be interior ones: a blockage caused by a continuing deep resentment against someone, falling wonderfully in love, an unhealthy obsession, fresh confidence because of a new job, a struggle with the black dog of depression, and so on. And always we have to reckon with the influence of our own type of personality, which will have a significant effect on our spiritual journey (see next chapter). In other words, other factors may have to be taken into account in planning a new move spiritually. But having said all that, **how do we want to move on?** The future is ours – and God's.

What now?

All these four images – the mountain, the bowl, the border and the journey – are intended to provide space for self-understanding so that we can say, 'This is where I think I've got to in my Christian life.' And in many cases we may have found we have lost our way a bit, or got rather tired, or maybe

Figure 2

even ground to a halt. A secular culture would say, 'Then give it up! There are lots of easier ways to live.' It may feel as if we are driving slowly along country lanes, with steep hills, dangerous corners, fallen trees and wandering wildlife, while a few hundred yards away all the other drivers are streaming effortlessly down a six-lane motorway. Remember, though, that Jesus had a bit to say about wide and narrow roads that lead to different destinations (Matthew 7.13)!

The purpose of this book is to offer a variety of ways in which we can resume the spiritual journey with greater confidence and purpose. There is a huge store of Christian resources available to us, and most of us have only just begun to explore them. This is an invitation to a richer exploration.

They said that

Once we've met Jesus and heard the music of the spheres, we can never be the same again.   ANON

Remember a principle which both gives us a firm rock and leaves us maximum elasticity for our minds. The principle: hold fast to Christ, and for the rest be totally uncommitted   HERBERT BUTTERFIELD

Abbot Lot went to Abbot Joseph and said: 'Father, according as I am able I keep my little rule and my little fast, my prayer, meditation and contemplative silence; and according as I am able I strive to cleanse my heart of thoughts; now what more should I do?' Abbot Joseph rose up in reply and stretched out his hands to heaven and said, 'Why not be totally changed into fire?'   THE DESERT FATHERS

I don't know who – or what – put the question. I don't know when it was put. I don't even remember answering. But at some moment I did answer Yes to Someone – or Something – and from that hour I was certain that existence is meaningful and that therefore, my life, in self-surrender, had a goal.   DAG HAMMARSKJOLD

There is usually some carefully guarded no-entry zone which has to be breached in us, some proud tower which has to be torn down. The pride of intellect, some reserve or polite control of our nature, some carefully formed attitude: whatever it is, it has to go. Ask God to show you what your [no-entry zone] is; what it is that has to be surrendered; where it is that a breach in the fortification of the self must be made; what in you must be humbled and brought low. Then make the act of surrender, wherever you are, and allow God to take your life.   RICHARD HOLLOWAY

Give me a point where I may stand and I will move the world.
ARCHIMEDES

I am a Christian only because of Jesus Christ, and for no other conscious reason. I find him unforgettable. I cannot get him out of my system. I do not know how he got there, but I am thankful that he did. I am a Christian because of Jesus Christ, especially because of the way he lived, and the way he died, what his death did, and what he did with death in resurrection.   DOUGLAS WEBSTER

We must stand for something lest we fall for anything.
TOC H PRAYER BOOK

2 Beginning again with prayer

Before we start

Before we start to look at a number of different ways of being in touch with the living God in prayer, a few things need to be thought about. Why is prayer so important? What is at the heart of prayer? How does my way of praying relate to my own personality?

Why is prayer so important?

To ask the question 'why pray?' is a bit like asking the question 'why breathe?' One is essential to physical life; the other is essential to spiritual life. We pray to stay alive as Christians. We breathe the oxygen of God's presence and love. To be more specific:

* We pray in order to share our lives with God. If we are trying to put him at the centre of our lives we have to keep the doors open to his constant arrival.

* We pray in order to get to know God. How do you get to know another country? You go and live there. Prayer is living with God in a new country with new priorities, and we live with him there in order to become acclimatized to the new culture of the kingdom of God.

* We pray in order to express our love and thanks to God. When 'deep calls to deep' within us, prayer is one of our responses, reaching to God with the heart. A relationship with God ought to have fewer of the characteristics of duty and more of the characteristics of a love affair.

* We pray as a way of loving people. Because we love them we pray

for them. The most important thing we can do for those we care for is to hold them in the loving presence of God.

✴ We pray to bring our own needs to God. Yes, that's OK too!

What is at the heart of prayer?

People often get anxious about prayer. It becomes associated with very holy people in monasteries, or with mastering complicated techniques which make you look pale and rather ill. One simple way of understanding the heart of prayer is that it's a relationship, and shares many of the characteristics of other relationships.

In a marriage, for example, you might say there are four levels of relating – 'just getting on with it', chatting, talking and intimacy.

✴ **'Just getting on with it.'** A lot of married life is not lived with the conscious thought that you are married; rather, you get on with the business of living, but against the constant backdrop of being a married person. So in a relationship with God, much of it is lived out in the rough and tumble of getting the children off to school, emptying the bins and trying to keep up with *EastEnders*. But it is none the less real for that. If God cannot be in the midst of the damp and drizzle of ordinary life, there is not much value in a guest appearance on Sundays.

✴ **Chatting.** Much married life is spent with fairly functional levels of communication. 'Can you remember to pick up some milk on the way home?' 'I've got to take the car in for a service.' 'Guess whose birthday we forgot last week?' It is not the stuff of dreams, but it is the stuff of families which function well. So with God, we often raise our thoughts or thanks or crises to him in the briefest of ways, but absolutely rightly, because this is how we are and this is how we feel.

✴ **Talking.** No marriage can survive without some communication which gets under the surface and involves each person concentrating on the other. Some academic study turned up the happy little fact that the average couple spent two minutes per day in this kind of deeper communication! But this is the time for communicating our feelings, hopes and anxieties, and responding thoughtfully to family events, work problems or other deeper issues. In the same way, in prayer, this is the time we set aside, short or long, and in very many different ways (as we shall see), simply to be with God. This is often where the problems start because we get tied up in knots trying to pray in ways which don't suit us.

* **Intimacy.** People need loving and most of us need loving a lot! Marriages involve intimacy, both emotionally and physically, and there is a level of communication where words fall away and the senses take over. This is the deepest level of communion between human beings, and it is not therefore surprising that there is a parallel in our communion with God. Ultimately, one might say, God is to be loved, and there are forms of prayer – for example, Christian meditation, silence, speaking in tongues – which allow us to do just that.

In the various styles of prayer which follow you will find that most of them correspond with one level or other of these strata of communication. All are valid. All are probably useful at some time or other in our life of prayer, but all of us are likely to find some levels of relating to God easier than others. That's the way it is because that's how we are made!

How does my way of prayer relate to my personality?

The way we pray will be influenced by a cluster of factors. Some of them are: the way we were brought up and our early formative experiences as Christians; the theology we perhaps unconsciously work with; the culture and historical moment of which we are part. But one of the most important factors, and one not properly recognized until recently, is the make-up of our personality. We actually need to pray 'with the grain' of our personalities, not against them. As has been said often, we need to pray as we can, not as we can't.

Sometimes, however, things have been against us. For example, we may have been brought up to pray or read the Bible in a certain way and because we cannot do it, or sustain it or find it life-giving, we feel a failure and wonder what is wrong with us. I suspect many a faith journey has been aborted because people were told authoritatively how to conduct themselves as Christians in prayer and other matters, and found that they simply could not do it, so gave up the struggle. And yet our God is so rich! He loves and cherishes every personality type for the very good reason that he made it. The great thing is that there are ways of being with him in prayer which are appropriate to every personality type.

The study of personality is, of course, immensely complex. Psychologists, biologists, philosophers, poets and others will all have their own descriptive tools. We need, therefore, to beware of over-simplification when we are thinking about personality type. In what follows I am simply borrowing from one specific set of tools which many people have found helpful, and indeed I am only using one or two ideas from this particular toolbag. I make no ultimate claims for them, only that they have proved valuable.

A lot of work has been done recently on the link between prayer and personality, and there is a list of excellent studies in the Further Reading section at the end of the book. For the moment let us just note that one useful tool has been the Myers-Briggs Personality Type Indicator which is based on Jungian psychological types. Through this approach we can recognize certain dominant functions in our personalities and each will have a considerable effect on the way we most comfortably pray.

For example, if the **senses** exert a dominant influence it may be that we favour an immediate kind of sprituality, earthy, straightforward, and able to find God in the 'sacrament of the present moment'. We will tend to be loyal to our church, without agonizing much about it, valuing clarity in the services and the shape of the church's year, particularly the strong narrative of Holy Week. We enjoy having the right atmosphere and environment for worship, with good music and lighting, appropriate symbols and a warm church! Holy Communion is particularly meaningful for us, and maybe Mark's Gospel is a favourite with its immediacy and directness. We may also like to meet God in his creation, in birdsong and the smell of newly cut grass.

On the other hand if our **intuition** is a dominant influence in our personality we may find that we are attracted by a more opaque, reflective form of spirituality. We may like to muse with God, and see his presence permeating the world mysteriously but excitingly, so that there is always the possibility of change and the dreaming of dreams. God is a God of constant surprises, who can't be held down but is always bringing new things into being. Worship therefore needs to have an element of openness, reflective-ness and mystery. Early morning communion may appeal to us but worship can easily become barren if it is mundane. Contemplative prayer might also appeal, and St John's Gospel is likely to be a favourite.

A third personality type has **thinking** as the dominant function and so faith tends to be rational, logical, honest, and concerned about truth and justice. Worship and prayer are rather objective, even impersonal in style, and such people can be alienated by too much emotion (like sharing the Peace, liturgical dance, or charismatic worship). We will like good, thoughtful sermons and sensible, carefully prepared intercessions. Bible

17

reading will be important but will require intelligent study, not just a comforting message in Bible-reading notes. However we may also have deep emotions ourselves, not easily expressed, and the perfectionism in us may make us interested in the mystical tradition of prayer. We may feel a little marginalized in the church, thinking that our emphases are overlooked. Matthew's Gospel may be a favourite because of its clarity, theological coherence and emphasis on teaching.

Finally there is a personality type where **feelings** are dominant. The emphasis in this spirituality is on intimacy with God and with other Christians and on warm, deeply felt prayer. Harmony in the church is very important and we will work hard to reconcile people, even taking the blame on to ourselves when problems occur. The cross is therefore an influential theological theme. Prayer will be heartfelt and warm, emphasizing forgiveness, compassion and joy, but also the love which may find it has to suffer. God is seen as shepherd and Father, infinitely forgiving. The Prodigal Son is a favourite parable; indeed Luke is a much-loved Gospel with its sensitivity to women and outsiders and its emphasis on healing. Holy Communion too is important because it embodies the suffering which led to reconciliation and the restoration of intimacy between God and his people. Daily prayer and quiet space are essential because we could easily dry up like a thirsty plant in a dry land.

Perhaps you can recognize a glimmering of where 'home' might be for you in those very brief descriptions. They are not intended to box us in. Indeed we will probably recognize parts of each one of these descriptions as true for us. But we start with natural preferences ('home') and can then go off on journeys of exploration, bringing home new experiences and discoveries. There is a huge amount more which could be said in this area but it is sufficient now to point out how differently we may approach the simple word 'prayer'.

It follows therefore that what we need is something of an à la carte menu in starting or restarting to pray. The various styles of prayer outlined on the following pages will appeal to different people at different times. Please experiment with different styles because in fact we sometimes pray out of our 'shadow', that is, those parts of our personality which are less influential – but that's another story!

It might help to start with, however, if we noted the links between personality types as explained above and the approaches to prayer which follow in the rest of this chapter. Again, don't be restricted by this; it is only an initial signpost.

Dominant **senses**	Try: ACTS/TCP
	One to One: Daily Office
	Taking a walk with God
	Triggers
Dominant **intuition**	Try: Imaginative prayer
	Meditation
	Silence
Dominant **thinking**	Try: One to One: Daily Office
	Silence
	Jesus Prayer
Dominant **feeling**	Try: Arrows/listening to music
	Imaginative prayer
	Meditation
	Group prayer

You might also remember that prayer can easily be seen as an introverted kind of activity, one which appeals more to those who look inside themselves for their sources of energy. Of course an equal number of people are extroverted and look for their sources of energy and life outside themselves, in relationships with others. In what follows there is, therefore, an important section called 'Prayer for extroverts'.

One last thought: prayer is ultimately not my project but God's gift. If he breaks all the rules, that's just fine by me! For some people none of what follows about prayer may quite fit because God just comes and takes hold of them when he wants, and draws them into himself as he chooses. Well, blessed be God forever!

METHODS OF PRAYER

Structured prayer

Background

Some of us prefer to have a clear shape to our prayers so that we have a framework which sustains and guides us. We know then that we are covering the ground and we know where we are up to. It means we don't have to start with a blank screen every time we pray, and it keeps us on track in our prayers even when praying is becoming hard work.

Many other people, for whom this would not necessarily be a first choice of prayer, also find it useful to have this as a fall-back and a place of safety.

What to do

1 **ACTS.** Order your time of prayer by using this simple and much-taught mnemonic:

Adoration: look to God and delight in him and in his presence. Let the sheer wonder of his huge mercy, beauty and love seep into your soul. Perhaps use a favourite Bible verse to lead you in:

* O Lord, our Lord, how majestic is your name in all the earth! (Psalm 8.1).

* The earth is the Lord's and all that is in it, the world and those who live in it. (Psalm 24.1)

* 'My Lord and my God!' (John 20.28)

Confession: bring to God the actions, and more often, the thoughts of the heart, which you know to have been off-beam. Perhaps you could run a video recording of the previous 24 hours before your mind and spot the problems! Occasional lapses are less important than patterns of behaviour and seemingly intractable attitudes. This should not become an orgy of guilt, but rather be an honest facing of personal realities.

Thanksgiving: no need to be too grandiose – start with the everyday, the fresh water in the shower, the sunlight on the roofs, the day's first smile. That will lead on to more major gifts and pleasures which are tumbling out of the hands of God all the time. Thanksgiving is a lovely, ever-expanding experience; in fact it becomes quite habit forming! The more we give thanks, the more we find there is to give thanks for.

Supplication is the last on the list, but so often this is all that people think prayer actually is – just asking God to fix things for us. In fact supplication is a way of loving. It means caring enough for people and situations that we take them to God and put them in his hands. The needs of the world, of the community, of our church, our friends, ourself – all are infinite, and some control needs to be exercised about how much we take on in prayer. Prayer lists help some, while others find they induce guilt! For further ideas see my book *The Intercessions Handbook* (SPCK, 1997), pp 152–3.

2 An alternative to ACTS is **TCP**, standing for **thanksgiving, confession, petition** (asking). This may be simpler for those of us for whom adoration is too demanding a point of entry, and who have a visual memory which includes little bottles of antiseptic! TCP is easy to remember and easy to take. Yet another alternative is **PRAY**, standing for **praise, repent, ask, yield**, which ends with opening ourselves up to God for him to use and to fill with his Spirit.

3 **Five-finger exercise.** Another simple and memorable method is to use the hand as an aid to prayer. Each finger can represent an area of life to pray for.

* Index finger (the finger that points). pray for the people who guide and help us either personally or in schools, churches, and community.

* Middle finger (the tallest finger): pray for those in government, international affairs, business, the media and other positions where important decisions are taken.

* Ring finger (the weakest finger): pray for those who can do little by themselves but depend on the compassion of others – the ill, the bewildered, the hungry.

* Little finger (the modest finger): representing ourselves (on a good day!).

* The thumb (the strongest of the five): pray for the most significant things in our lives such as family, home and work.

And remember that we are always kept 'in the palm of God's hand' (Isaiah 49.16).

4 **Prayer books.** Some books of prayers lend themselves to regular use as a structured form of prayer. These are not the ordinary books of prayers which are intended to be mined by those who are leading prayers in public worship. They are the kind which have an extended shape of meditation and prayer for each day and so can be used for a complete period of prayer. Eddie Askew has been producing books of this kind published by the Leprosy Mission for some years, containing a scripture meditation and related prayer. So too a very helpful book by Ruth Etchells called *Just As I Am* (Triangle 1994), offers extended prayer morning and evening, drawing also on the reflections and prayers of others. A wander through a Christian bookshop will turn up a number of book of meditations and prayers which can function in this way, or which can provide a springboard for personal prayer.

One to one; a simple Daily Office

Background

Large numbers of Christians all over the world have used the format of prayer known as the Daily Office. Indeed ordained clergy in many churches are expected to say Morning and Evening Prayer every day. An Office is a service from the old monastic tradition of prayers which punctuated the day. It contains psalms, biblical readings and prayers and now, in various forms, provides the framework for many people seeking a structured approach to prayer.

One of the big advantages of an Office is that it carries you along whether you feel like praying or not. It provides a comprehensive offering of prayer and exposure to scripture, so that in a sense you know you have been fed whether you have responded to the food or not. What we are doing in 'saying the Office' is joining our prayers to the prayers of the whole church, rather like putting our drop of water into the huge river of prayer forever flowing towards the Lord our God.

Morning and Evening Prayer are prominent in Anglican service books and have found a new popularity through the publication of the Franciscan *Celebrating Common Prayer* (Mowbray 1992). Sometimes, however, these forms of the Office are too long or complex for the lay Christian, and simpler Offices have been devised. What follows is one particular form of the Office which can be adapted to suit the needs of lay people who like the idea of structure but are unsure about taking on the fuller, more complex forms of Daily Office.

One to One

INTRODUCTION

Lord open my lips
   and my mouth shall proclaim your praise.
Lord come and help me.
   Lord, support and save me.

PSALM FOR THE DAY

Taken from the lectionary, a cycle of daily readings and psalms published each year by SPCK. Alternatively take a new psalm each day, but limit yourself to 20–25 verses of the longer psalms.

READING FOR THE DAY

✳ Taken from the lectionary or use ideas from the Bible section of this book.

✳ Followed by silent meditation.

PRAYER

Perhaps ACTS or TCP or imaginative prayer (see elsewhere in this chapter).

THE OFFERING OF THE DAY

Lord, I offer this day to you: the work I do, the people I meet, the pleasures and the pains, that in everything I may know the love of Christ, and be thankful.

✳ Silent offering of the day's concerns and activities.

The Lord's Prayer

CONCLUDING PRAYER

Keep me, Lord, in the joy, the simplicity and the compassionate love of the gospel. Bless me this day, and those who you have given to my care, through Jesus Christ our Lord. Amen.

   The grace of our Lord Jesus Christ, the love of God, and the fellowship of the Holy Spirit, be with the whole church evermore. Amen.

Praying on the run

Background

For many people the idea of being able to carve out a regular time to set apart for prayer is simply unreal. Either it does not accord with their praying instincts, or they are at a stage in life where nappies, ironing and the school run are the overwhelming realities rather than the luxury of times for prayer and Bible reading.

It is very important that people are not made to feel guilty because they cannot do, or do not want to do, as the saints and heroines of the prayer group do! We are not dealing with different classes of spirituality; we are dealing with different personalities and different times of life.

For such people prayer is best done on the run. God is in the thick of things, so that is where he can be met. Length of time spent in prayer is of minor importance compared with integrity of prayer. The trouble is that the stereotype for holiness is an introvert with a lot of time on his hands. Books on prayer tend to have been written by such people, read by such people and passed on with fervour by such people! Others can feel like spiritual outsiders, with a GCSE 'fail' in Spirituality.

What such people need is confidence in their preferred ways of praying, and some good, fulfilling ways of opening themselves and their days to God, the God who, one suspects, is just as likely to be found in the hubbub of the supermarket and the classroom as in the ordered peace of the Lady Chapel and the prayer group.

What to do

1 **Arrows.** The great privilege of prayer is that we have instant access to the halls of heaven. So when we meet someone in need, or hear of someone with an illness, or have a difficult situation to face, or hear an ambulance siren in the distance, we can immediately take our concern to the God who knows the whole picture. An arrow prayer does not need careful composition or accurate grammar: simply, 'Lord, help her through this', 'Help, I'm stuck!', 'Lord, have mercy'. Our prayer may even be in our eyes and the way we look at people and situations – for we will see all of life in relation to God. Arrow

praying makes the day quite an adventure as we recognize people's needs and ask for the touch of Christ on their lives.

2 **Triggers.** Once our feet hit the bedroom carpet in the morning the day races away. But it has its own rhythms, rituals and repetitions. Some of them might act as triggers for us to press the pause button for a moment and to pray. When we turn on the tap we have a moment of waiting which can be used to pray; when we get in the car, or sit down at a desk, or wait at the lights – all these are points to pause. I find it helpful to pray for things associated with the trigger itself; for example, when turning on the tap, to pray for those who have no clean water without walking miles; and when sitting at the desk, to pray for those who cannot read or write in this country and in different parts of the world. However, these moments can be used for general prayer as well, for offering the day to God, or praying for the problems that family and friends may be facing that day. Moreover almost anything can trigger the prayer of thanksgiving: the tree in the front garden, the courage of a bereaved friend, the face of a child.

3 **The Jesus Prayer.** An ancient and much loved form of prayer from the Eastern Church is known as the Jesus Prayer. It consists of repeating the simple prayer, *'Lord Jesus Christ, Son of God, have mercy on me, a sinner.'* Some people repeat it regularly, over and over, finding that it focuses them on Jesus in the midst of life. Some pray it in time with their breathing: breathing in to the first two phrases of the prayer and out to the last two; breathing in the goodness of Jesus, and breathing out the negatives of our own lives. The Western Christian may hear the prayer as somewhat negative in tone but it is not heard that way in the Eastern Church. It merely expresses our total dependence on God in Christ and the mercy which undergirds all our lives. The effect is to let the life and Spirit of Christ infuse our lives, and we can pray in this way whenever and wherever we want. I have found it is particularly useful when waiting to see the dentist!

4 **Listening to music.** In an age of audio tapes it has become possible to pray in another way through a busy day. A tape of worship songs, or Taizé chants, or Iona music, or Rutter anthems can be played in a busy kitchen or a traffic jam. The music can bring calm joy into the middle of the everyday round of common tasks, and increase our awareness that God is never more than a thought away.

5 **Practising the presence of God.** A seventeenth-century French monk

who worked in the monastery kitchen coined this valuable phrase about praying through the day. He discovered as much delight in God's presence in his kitchen as in the chapel. The kitchen was a very busy place, as are our kitchens today, but he talked of finding God always and everywhere by simply being attentive to him, remembering him. This does not mean living three inches off the ground all the time. It means turning to God naturally and often, like tuning in to a radio station which is always transmitting programmes that are available to us whenever we want to be in touch. God's loving presence is always just a glance away. Another writer has called this way of living and praying 'living concurrently'. That is, we can be focused on two things at once – on what we are doing in ordinary life (working, relaxing, shopping,) as well as on God, just as a mother can be focused on her work at the same time as being completely attentive to the presence of a child playing nearby. Practising the presence of God is reminding ourselves of the ever-present divine love pressing gently upon our lives.

Taking a walk with God

Background

The last section on praying on the run was designed for the person who does not naturally settle down to a specific time of one-to-one prayer, and for the person who is at a stage in life which precludes that possibility. Another way of prayer which can help such people, as well as those who encounter God more easily in his created world than in buildings and books, is taking a prayerful walk.

I have a friend who is never closer to God than on a wild coast, where the strength and beauty of God is felt full-blown upon her face. My own response to mountains also has something of that spiritual quality – an encounter with a God of glory and splendour. But others find the morning walk with the dog through the park or fields is their time to talk things through with God. A walk to work can function in the same way.

What to do

There are no rules about any of this: whoever thought of making rules about a conversation with a friend? We set off and we talk with God about whatever is on our minds. Sometimes this might be the sheer delighted sharing of good things, sometimes the sharing of puzzles and problems. Sometimes there might be prayers of complaint ('It's no wonder you have so few friends!'); sometimes the silence of glad companionship.

Someone who prefers to meet God in the open air might be particularly liberated by the sight of a particular flower or a covering of leaves, the graceful lines of a tree, or the sun (occasionally!) warming the earth. These experiences may heighten our awareness of a God of extraordinary richness and colour, and draw from us a profound sense of wonder and gratitude. On other occasions it is a plod through damp grass, but God is present in misty days and darker hues as well as in brilliant sunshine and bright colours.

It is possible to develop the idea of walking with God a little further. I often find it helpful to have three conkers in my pocket in the autumn. When I walk along, with my hands plunged into my pockets, I encounter the conkers and may be moved to pray. Holding one conker encourages me to pray to God the Father in thanksgiving perhaps for the beauty around me, or for someone for whom the idea of 'father' has got very tarnished because of their upbringing. Holding on to two conkers could have me praying to Jesus Christ for his friendship and closeness to someone in need. When I hold three conkers I focus my prayers on the Holy Spirit, asking perhaps for my own life to be full of the Spirit's grace.

Walk with God (preferably a little more slowly than you might otherwise have done), and he will walk with you. And once we have recognized that he is present in our walking, we may realize that he never moves from our side, whatever we are doing.

Imaginative prayer

Background

Some people are helped to pray by having structures such as ACTS or a Daily Office. Others are cramped by such frameworks and need to let their imaginations loose. Such people are usually intuitive and employ their creative and instinctive natures more readily than their rational and ordering faculties. Prayer for them means space – space for journeys of the spirit, for gentle cogitation, and for leaps of the imagination.

Methods of prayer therefore need to give our spirits permission to explore. The following approaches are not meant to be limiting but to illustrate the possibilities of bringing the imagination to the fore. Some people have been brought up by their Christian tradition to be suspicious of the imagination as a merely human and subjective faculty which can lead us astray. It is certainly true that Christians are bound to the liberating truth of scripture which may need to correct our flights of fancy, but we also need to trust the 'baptized imagination' to be used by God in helping us to come close to him.

What to do

1 **Praying the day.** Imagine that the day past – or the day ahead, such as you can visualize is – is captured in a photograph album. Open the album and look at the pictures of all the things that have happened – the people you met, meetings you went to, jobs done, conversations, what you did by yourself, what you watched on television. All the time be aware of the inner story as well as the outer one – that is, what you were thinking and feeling about that event at the time and now. As you look at each snapshot, see it in the light and presence of God, so that you might want to be thankful for one scene and sorry about another; you might want to pray for that person you met over lunch and for that situation you heard about on the news; and to ask for strength to handle your tiresome friend better next time you meet. And so on. Every picture tells a story and every story can start a prayer. We just have to open the picture album.

2 **Encountering Jesus.** The essence of prayer for others is that we bring Jesus and that person together. One way of doing this is to use our visual imagination. We can imagine that we are bringing that person to meet Jesus, and then see it happening. It does not matter if we are unable to visualize Jesus with great clarity; that is often the case. What matters is that we bring the person there to Jesus and then step back out of the way.

No words need be exchanged since Jesus knows the person's situation fully. We can therefore watch as Jesus meets the person in whatever way seems right. Jesus may gently lay hands on the person, in an embrace, a touch, or a formal laying on of hands. We should try not to force the pace in any way but to let the encounter unfold in whatever way it will. Then watch as Jesus lets the person go.

There is great intimacy in this form of prayer, and therefore a lot of emotional energy may be expended in just bringing one or two people to Jesus in this way.

3 **Living water.** One of the most powerful biblical pictures of Jesus' dealing with an individual in need is in the story of the Samaritan woman at the well (John 4.1–26). In that story he suggests that she might ask him and he would give her not the ordinary water she thought she needed but 'living water' which would be a spring of life inside her. This is an image which can be adapted helpfully in our praying for others.

We see the person we are praying for coming to the well, by the side of which stands Jesus ... we see them standing together ... Jesus knows fully that person's need ... he picks up a cup of water and offers it ... the cup is taken and the water drunk, living water, bringing healing, strength, forgiveness, peace, or the gift of life itself from the hands of Jesus ... any other exchange takes place between Jesus and the person we are praying for – a word, a touch, a blessing ... the person goes away renewed, refreshed, changed by Jesus.

Again the encounter can be quite draining emotionally and spiritually, but it should not be rushed. We are not there to manipulate but to observe. If we see another person brought to the well the exchange might be quite different. To the person who prays with the imagination this kind of approach will be much more meaningful than going through a list of names.

4 **Letting yourself be loved.** St Teresa of Avila had a favourite way of praying which can prove to be powerfully helpful to many. She spoke

of letting Jesus look at us. That's all! 'Notice him looking at you,' she said, but added the two very important words *lovingly and humbly*. This is what makes this way of praying so powerful. Many people have a low self-image and the idea of Jesus looking at *us* lovingly and humbly is almost too much to bear.

The basis of this form of praying of course is that Jesus came as a servant, one who washed feet and was prepared to die for love of us. He looks at us with the love of the cross and the humility of the towel. And if we can learn to accept his looking at us, that more than anything else will begin to build up our self-esteem, and enable us to look at others lovingly and humbly too.

This is not a way of prayer to be rushed.

5 **The caim.** The Celts had a characteristic way of praying by enfolding their family and community in the caim, which was the circle of God's protective care. Sometimes they would draw out the circle with their pointed finger, marking out the terrain of God's protection. This form of prayer seems to touch many people today with its vivid, bold symbolism.

We can pray simply by saying, 'Circle, Lord, your servant Kate with your endless love.' Or we can imagine a circle drawn around our immediate family, and then around our church, and then around our nation, and then around our world, and each time we can pray for those enclosed in the protective embrace of God's mercy. There are many ways we can use and adapt the idea of the caim. We might, for instance, employ the prayer by using our own finger to draw the circle as we pray. Or we might especially pray for the circling of the car with God's protection as we start a long journey. This won't give magical protection of course and we will still have to drive straight! Nevertheless, such prayer puts us in God's hands and helps us to use all our driving skill.

6 **Creative or artistic prayer.** Some of us may find it helpful to do something with our hands as we pray, rather than be imaginative just with our minds. If we are like that, we might like to write, draw or even doodle our prayers! We could write down the names of people we want to pray for, and then draw a circle of God's protection around them as we pray. Or we could draw them instead. I have sometimes asked people to pray and reflect on a theme by using children's modelling clay; the results are often striking and moving. Or we can get rid of sins and failures by writing them down and then

burning the paper so that our sins are removed far from us; but don't do this in a room with a smoke alarm! With a little imagination there are many ways to use artistic gifts and inclinations in prayer. How about writing poetry as an act of prayer, or journalizing your thoughts and prayers in a notebook? Let your creativity flow!

Meditation

Background

Some people are naturally more quiet and reflective in their praying. They do not feel at ease with too many words or too much intercession. They want to ponder the deep things of God and mull over their relationship with him. One of their natural ways of praying may well be meditation.

Meditation could be described as 'quiet *thinking* towards God'. That would distinguish it from contemplation which could be described as 'quiet *looking* towards God', but in practice the one often leads into the other, as we shall see when we come to the next section on silent prayer. Meditation is essentially chewing over verses from the Bible (or other writings) to taste the goodness of God revealed in them. It is a bit like sucking a favourite sweet and savouring the taste. It involves a process of thinking, but the thinking is always prayerful rather than analytical, the intention being to take us deeper into God himself rather than further into study of the text.

What to do

The process of *lectio divina*, holy reading, is more fully described in the next chapter under 'the Benedictine method' of Bible reading (page 53). It involves **reading** a verse or two until a phrase asks to be explored, then **thinking** about that phrase and repeating it attentively and lovingly, and then **praying** about the things which have emerged from the meditation. Joyce Huggett simplifies the process to the three stages: read, reflect, respond. Meditation gets under our mental guard because it makes us read the Bible in order to be nourished by it rather than to challenge it or argue with it. We do not leave our critical faculties outside the door but the intention is to stand under the text rather than over it.

Other books may also provide the substance for our meditation. The Christian heritage of holiness and spiritual wisdom is rich enough to be bewildering, but some books have stood the test of many generations of meditative reading and are worth noting. The point always is, however, not to read the book in order to be informed but to be transformed. It is to be taken in small portions, read slowly and thoughtfully (though probably not phrase by phrase as with the Bible), and then meditated on for as long as it takes.

Each one of us will develop our own list of special books and God is gloriously free to use whatever he wants to speak to us, but we might note these below. In this century there are many books which are ideal for meditation. The selection below gives just a taste of the range and variety of different wells from which we can now drink.

* Henri Nouwen, *The Genesee Diary* (DLT 1995). One of many excellent books from this Dutch Catholic priest, this one using a helpful diary format.

* Brother Roger of Taizé, *His Love Is a Fire* (Geoffrey Chapman/ Mowbray 1990). Writings from the journal of the founder of this ground-breaking community. Refreshing and incisive.

* Anthony de Mello, *The Song of the Bird* (Doubleday Image 1984). Thought-provoking stories and parables from a much-read spiritual writer.

* David Adam, *The Cry of the Deer* (Triangle 1987). One of many books of Celtic prayers and reflections by this writer.

* Thomas Kelly, *A Testament of Devotion* (HarperCollins 1992). A modern spiritual classic from an American Quaker.

* There are many books of the 'Through The Year With . . .' variety. These can be very helpful if somewhat 'low-fat' in terms of richness.

* Books of poetry such as *The Lion Christian Poetry Collection* are often first-rate for meditation because poems are usually short and packed with thought.

Behind these modern writings, however, is a tradition of spiritual classics which has fed countless Christians through the centuries. They should never be dismissed as outdated or out of touch, any more than the Bible should be. They speak of eternal issues with perennial power.

* St Augustine, *Confessions*. Classic account of his journey to conversion and beyond

* Thomas à Kempis, *The Imitation of Christ*. The way of a follower of Christ, written in the fifteenth century and engaging with perennial problems.

* Julian of Norwich, *Revelations of Divine Love*. Mystical writing from the Middle Ages describing the sixteen visions of an engaging and lively personality.

There are scores more where these came from. For some they will be too quaintly located in another age. For others they will be like coming home.

Books of readings, Lent books, study courses, collections, anthologies and other devotional books are published with somewhat alarming regularity. We have to be discerning about what will really help us at our own particular point on the journey, and realize that with such a lot of titles appearing, few of them will ever attain 'classic' status.

Again, the important point is not just to read these books as one would read a novel, but to take short sections and to chew them ruminatively, as a cow chews a cud – with steady rhythm and determination! Then the riches of the world's spiritual giants lie before us.

Silence

Background

When we start praying we may initially make quite a lot of noise. There is a lot to do, a lot to try and a lot to say. Gradually, however, some people find that there comes a thirst to be quieter. They want to still the noise, both around them and within them, in order to listen to the quiet thunder of the Lord of Hosts. Often people begin to meditate on scripture, to turn over in the mind and heart some verses of the Bible and so to find a new nourishment in prayer. Sometimes people want to become quieter still because they find words a distraction; they thirst for an encounter with God beyond the limitations of language. They are drawn into silence.

Sometimes the prayer of silence has been called contemplation. That is fine as long as it does not sound as if it is only for people with an honours degree in spirituality and sainthood. Contemplation, or silent prayer, is a quiet looking towards God, a gentle longing, a reaching out in the darkness. There are no success criteria with this form of prayer, nothing to 'achieve'; being there and looking towards God is enough. A famous encounter took place between a French priest and a simple parishioner he saw day after day sitting in church looking at the crucifix. 'What are you doing?' the priest eventually asked him. 'Well,' said the man, nodding to the figure of Christ on the cross, 'I look at him and he looks at me, and we are happy together.'

What to do

* You may come across pools of silence forming naturally in the course of other times of prayer. Perhaps you find you want to stop and wait and enjoy the stillness. You may be experiencing a call to explore silence more deliberately.

* If you are intentional about silence you may want to start with just a couple of minutes, but this may extend to five or ten minutes, and then fifteen or longer, if the time is available. A silent prayer group may give thirty minutes or an hour to silence. There is no right or wrong amount of time in silent prayer.

* It helps to have a way of quietening the mind gradually, like a car

leaving the motorway and slowing up towards the junction. One way is this:

- commit the time to God, who is present and waiting

- still the body, relax the shoulders, let the tension seep away

- listen to the sounds around you, be they distant, close by or within

- open yourself to God.

* It then helps to have a phrase of scripture, or even a word, to act as your initial focus and the place to return to if you get lost or distracted. It may be a longer phrase: 'The Lord is my strength and my song', 'Be still and know that I am God', 'Taste and see that the Lord is good', 'As the deer longs for the running waters, so my soul longs for you, O God'. Or the phrase may be shorter: 'Jesus, my Lord', 'The light of the world', 'Lord, have mercy', 'You, Lord, only'. Start by repeating the phrase slowly and lovingly in order to enter it properly and to let it enter you. As the words become less important just repeat the phrase as and when necessary.

* Then simply stay in the silence and let happen what will. You are opening yourself to God, not to a particular experience of him. There is nothing to 'get through' and nothing to 'get out'. You are there for God as he is there for you. You may experience little or nothing 'holy' but that does not mean God is not dealing with the soul, and you will probably find that in spite of everything, you are needing more and more to spend time in silence.

* Yes, you may be bored and wish the allotted time was up, and then feel guilty for such an unholy thought! No matter; turn back to the phrase; look towards God. Or you may be plagued by distractions, a hundred irritants which turn up unexpected and unasked. Again, no matter; turn back to the phrase; look towards God. On the other hand, you might also like to entertain those distractions for a while and ask God why they are there. What do those particular thoughts mean? They have presumably been kept in our mental cellar and it is only the silence which is allowing them to come out to play. There can be a rich source here of personal reflection and growth, particularly in a society which discourages quietness and the subversive whisper of the Spirit.

* Another helpful focus in the prayer of silence is the gentle light of a candle. Its quiet persistence, its supple movement, and its fragile strength, are all aids to inner stillness. Or you might like to hold on to a hand-cross, or a stone (your uniqueness, your resilience, but also perhaps your hardness of spirit). Or to look at an icon and then, through that, to the depths of the divine.

* It is a common experience that silent prayer in a group rather than alone has a particular quality and intensity. We are bound together in mutual support and a common focus, and the result may be a profound stillness and openness to God.

* Silence is not easy. It requires patience and discipline, but for many people it is the answer to a deep thirst; it opens the gate of glory like nothing else can.

A pilgrim had been listening to a famous spiritual teacher. He said to one of the teacher's followers: 'I've travelled a long way to listen to the teacher but I really find his words quite ordinary.' 'Don't listen to his words,' said the follower, 'listen to his message.' 'How do I do that?' came the response. 'Take hold of a sentence that he says,' said the other, 'shake it well until all the words drop off, and what you have left will set your heart on fire.'

Prayer for extroverts

Background

Praying could easily seem to be more of an introverted activity than an extroverted one. In other words, it could appeal more to those who look inside themselves for their sources of energy than to those who are energized by being with other people. An extrovert might look at someone kneeling in prayer and apparently absorbed in their relationship with the Almighty, with something akin to alarm. 'Do I have to do *that*?' Someone starts talking about prayer in an intense, personal way and the extrovert often begins to feel guilty. He or she is persuaded to go on a church retreat, but has to pack a radio for fear of sinking unnoticed under the quicksands of silence. All the books on prayer can seem to be written by people who live from the inside out: notice how many of them seem to have titles like 'Out of the Depths', 'The Fire Within', 'The Desert in the Heart'.

There are, of course, just as many people who live from the outside in, who draw their energy from the external world of stimuli, of meeting people and dealing with everyday situations. The church must not disenfranchise them in its teaching on prayer and its way of praying. God is their God and prayer is their privilege, just as much as for any other person, but they are often left with a vague sense of dis-ease and guilt, as if they do not quite fit the mould.

Let's re-empower the extroverts!

What to do

1 **Christian living.** Praying for extroverts probably starts with taking seriously that splendid advice in Colossians: 'Whatever you do, in word or deed, *do everything* in the name of the Lord Jesus, giving thanks to God the Father through him' (Colossians 3.17). The emphasis is on doing, and doing for Christ. The actions of the day can themselves be an offering to God as they are done *for* him, as part of our God-given responsibility to be creative citizens. If the day's work is seen in that light it may not need a focused time of prayer; the prayer is in the holy living, the giving of everything to God. The focused prayer may simply be at the start of the day when

it is all offered to God ('Whatever I do, in word or deed . . .'), and at the end of the day when it is all gathered up into God again in gratitude ('giving thanks to God the Father . . .').

2 **Loving action.** One particular form of Christian living is when we act in love and care for people we know, meet, or are led to. When we are listening to a bereaved person pouring out their heart, or washing the wasted body of an elderly relative, or playing with a traumatized child, or collecting for Christian Aid Week, we are engaged in the love and service of Christ himself (see Matthew 25.31–46 where Jesus said 'Whatever you do for the least of my brothers and sisters you do for me'). We are meeting Christ in the other person. When St Francis or Mother Teresa cared for the sick and dying they saw their actions as a form of prayer, for if prayer is 'being with God' in certain ways (for example, thankfully, sorrowfully, or with people on our hearts) then loving action is certainly 'being with Christ' in practical care for his needy people. The prayer is the loving action, offered to God.

3 **Meeting Christ in the community.** Another form of prayer may be not just meeting Christ in the other person, as above, but meeting Christ in the community. If we take the image of the church as the body of Christ seriously (1 Corinthians 12) we are sharing the life of Christ as we share the life of the Christian community. When we are committed to the health and growth of the body of Christ we are loving and serving Christ himself, and that is at least one worthwhile description of prayer. To be a committed member of the church, helping it to celebrate its life and to obey its call, is to put flesh on to the bones of prayer. Let's get stuck in!

4 **Praying with others.** Extroverts are energized by being with other people. It follows therefore that they are often more at home praying with others than praying by themselves. An introvert is likely to think that when Jesus said 'Where two or three are gathered together in my name, there am I in the midst of them', he was referring to a maximum number of participants! The extroverts may think otherwise. Such a person may find that a prayer partner or prayer triplet, met every one or two weeks, will keep their praying up to the mark. There will be a sharing of real concerns, the experience of mutual support and accountability, encouragement in seeing how God is answering prayer – as well as a cup of coffee and a chat! A larger prayer group may also encourage rich, expectant prayer, as well as the opportunity to explore a variety of more imaginative ways of praying.

5 **Prayer in public worship.** Every church service will be in itself an
extended prayer, and will include within it a period of focused prayer.
This can be an encouragement to the extrovert's praying because it
offers the experience of coming before God together, in corporate
expectation and dependence. The 'success' or otherwise of the main
Sunday service can therefore be of major importance to those of us
whose lives are orientated outwards, because this is the main
experience of spiritual substance in the week. Introverts can always go
back to their own personal prayer life; extroverts need this occasion to
be good. However, if the family celebration on Sunday is full of life,
extroverts are well set up for the following week and for the practical
outworking of their faith.

6 **Quiet space.** The paradox in all this advice about prayer for extroverts
is that often it is precisely such people who you then find looking for
stillness and quiet! Just because they are living so much with this
'outward directedness', when it comes to prayer some find that what
they now want is quiet space. What is going on here is that the so-
called 'shadow' part of our personality is wanting to get a look in.
The opposite sides of our more dominant characteristics ask to be
allowed to grow so that we become overall more rounded and
complete in ourselves. It works the other way round as well of
course. The introvert is suddenly found at large Christian holiday
weeks learning how to do spiritual line-dancing! *C'est la vie spirituelle!*

The Small Print: when, where, with what?

In order to pray in several of the ways described above there is a need to
identify a particular time and place for prayer, and some practicalities about
it. This does not apply to 'praying on the run', 'taking a walk with God', or
'praying for extroverts', but it does apply to other forms of prayer when we
want to get down to business. Here are some practical pointers, to be used or
ridiculed as you find most helpful.

When?

* Who knows? Only you can know what time of day or night suits you
to pray. But it is undeniably a question of priorities. If prayer is as
much the lifeblood or the oxygen of the Christian life as I have

suggested, then we cannot be too busy to pray; we can only fail to make it a priority. So an element of self-discipline is necessary, just as it is to become proficient at computing or athletics.

* One obvious time for prayer is early in the day. Getting up twenty minutes earlier could be the answer. It then becomes a case of the 'victory of mind over mattress!' However, it may all be a madhouse around you at that time, so what about twenty minutes after lunch? Or after the children have been taken to school? Or last thing at night? The danger then, of course, is the critical angle at which you lie in bed; hunker down too far and you will be asleep before God knows you are there! Experiment; but don't give up.

* Parents of young children need a special word of encouragement and absolution. This is the most difficult time of life for any routine. It may be best to try the ideas in 'praying on the run', or praying as you walk round the supermarket, or as you change the nappy! Practise the presence of God, and be gentle with yourself.

* One important prop is regularity. Praying should become as regular and necessary as cleaning your teeth (though less mundane). We rarely debate with ourselves whether we should clean our teeth today. The answer is obvious; it is simply what we do. So with prayer.

* When people ask how long they should pray for, there is no obvious answer. Some people need just a short time to remind themselves and God that all is well; others need a long period of silent prayer. I have yet to have anyone disprove my promise that 'ten minutes a day with God will change your life'. But I also take comfort from Michael Ramsey's reply to a question about how long he had prayed for that day: 'One minute,' he said, 'but it took me twenty-nine minutes to get there.' Prayer is about quality, not quantity.

Where?

* For most people, having a special place to pray is basic. It might be a chair in a bedroom or by a window in the lounge or by the stove in the kitchen; it might be a church near our workplace, or even our car in the regular commuter traffic jam. It is then a place which is associated with prayer and we do not have to overcome its other (secular?) use each time we go to pray. We are halfway into prayer already, just by going there.

* This place then develops its own sense of presence. T. S. Eliot wrote of a place where 'prayer is made valid'. Place is an important spiritual concept. We all probably already have some sacred places, be they special mountains or seashores, or great cathedrals or little country churches.

* The Desert Fathers of the early church wrote of our special place as a 'cell'. 'Stay in your cell,' they said, 'and your cell will teach you everything.' We might instead call it a chapel. If we have been to our chapel regularly then we will carry it in our heart all day long.

With what?

* The answer is – anything that seems right. What we take into our time of prayer is as personal as the rest of our spiritual footprint. We may find helpful a Bible (certainly), but also a cross, a candle, an icon, a vase of small flowers, a picture of something significant, a cassette with music, books of meditations, an intercessions list – all sorts! One of my most helpful artefacts is a sculptured pair of hands I bought on the island of Patmos. I find I identify with the openness, the vulnerability and the sense of offering expressed in the beautiful shape of those hands.

* A simple prayer stool where you tuck your legs under the cross-piece on which you sit can be a comfortable way of being attentive. They are easily made, or bought. Ask around.

* Lighting a candle when we pray is no longer a statement about our church tradition. It simply marks out the time we are giving over to this special purpose. It sets the time apart. Moreover it is full of potential meaning in itself – the light of Christ, the living flame of faith, the warmth of God's abiding love.

* Our eyes might like to focus on that candle, or on a cross (which offers food for endless meditation), or on an icon, which can be used as a window through to the mystery of God.

* Just a few books for meditation may be kept near, but should be prevented from cluttering the place up. It should be a restful place, associated with restoration and peace. It might be helpful to have a notebook there also to act as a journal. In it you can record thoughts, ideas, experiences, impressions, and a narrative of your spiritual

journey. The act of writing is itself helpful, and reading it back weeks later can be very encouraging too, as we see what God has been doing in and around us.

✳ If you respond to music, a small CD/cassette player can give you the option of centring down in prayer with the aid of carefully chosen music. The choice today is huge, from modern choruses to Taizé chants, from Iona music to classical compilations. Just look in a Christian bookshop.

✳ Above all, the Bible will be our constant companion in our time of prayer. Here is the written word which leads us to the living Word. We are lost without it.

They said that

Prayer is being present to the presence of God.   JOHN V. TAYLOR

Prayer is keeping company with God.   ST CYRIL OF ALEXANDRIA

Prayer is laying hold of God's willingness, not overcoming his reluctance.   ANON

Prayer is listening to the heartbeat of God.   ANON

In prayer you put yourself with God, empty perhaps, but hungry and thirsty for him; and if in sincerity you cannot say that you want God you can perhaps tell him that you want to want him; and if you cannot say even that, perhaps you can say that you want to want to want him!   MICHAEL RAMSEY

I have so much to do today that I must spend several hours in prayer before I am able to do it.   JOHN WESLEY

If the question 'what is the use of prayer?' means only 'does it produce the goods?', the questioner has abandoned the sphere of religion for that of the market place.   PETER BAELZ

I believe that prayer makes things change, but there's no guarantee which things. Sometimes prayer changes me – I can cope with things I dreaded, for instance. Sometimes prayer reaches another person and helps him or her cope in a new way. Sometimes events change their course. It's not a yes–no situation. It's opening myself out and discovering that there is a love beyond my own to see me through.   MICHAEL HARE-DUKE

The right relation between prayer and conduct is not that conduct is supremely important and prayer helps it, but that prayer is supremely important and conduct tests it.   WILLIAM TEMPLE

It is true that we must pray as we can and not as we can't, but it is also true that the self's innate tendency is to settle for minimalist prayer, which always gives up at the point of the beginning of discomfort. No growth in prayer is possible without some venture into pain.
RICHARD HOLLOWAY

The meaning of prayer is that we get hold of God, not of the answer.   OSWALD CHAMBERS

Paul and I were late for a meeting and urgently needed a bus to get there. So we sat down by the side of the road, closed our eyes and prayed that the Lord would send a bus. As our eyes were shut, the bus went past. The scriptural motto for this experience is 'watch and pray'.   MURRAY WATTS

3 Beginning again with the Bible

Practicalities

When we come to the Bible we are not just reading a story; we are being dealt with by God. In this book we are encountering the living word of a lively God, and our task is not to stand in judgement on it but to stand under its judgement on us. We find however that its judgement is full of mercy for, in fact, this is a glorious love story – the story of a loving God pursuing his wayward people to give them back their birthright, which is 'life in all its fullness' (John 10.10).

How to start

Get a Bible! The version is important, however. There is still a strange presumption amongst some godparents that the newly baptized infant will clearly want his or her first experience of the Bible to be the Authorized Version (AV). The AV is an acquired taste for people today. The beauty of seventeenth-century English is undeniable, but the value of it for new Christians is limited. More likely are the Good News Bible (easy, readable style, restricted vocabulary), the New International Version (modern, classic style) or the New Revised Standard Version (inclusive, non-gender-specific language). The important thing is to have a look at the same passage in each version and see which one appeals.

Getting the background

It can be very valuable to have some basic notion of the overall biblical story, so that you know how various parts fit in with each other. The broadest understanding of the storyline will do at the moment but it saves a lot of embarrassment later on if we know where the Exodus fits in with the Exile, and where the Kings fit in with the Prophets. The easiest way to get hold of a storyline is from a book like the *Lion Handbook to the Bible* or some other modern, visual portrayal of the basics, including maps of the territory. Note immediately that the Bible was not written in the order that the books appear! Genesis was written late on, for example, and Paul's letters were written mostly before the Gospels. And so the fascinating world of Bible study emerges.

Starting to read

The first thing is not to start at Genesis. If you do you will probably grind to a halt somewhere in the middle of Leviticus! Get a feel for the different genres of the biblical material. After all, it was written over perhaps 1,400 years by over sixty writers in different cultures and for different reasons. It is a library of books including history, poetry, epic stories, prayers, love songs, gospel, law, letters, proverbs, prophecy, and more – but all bearing witness to the urgent, pressing beauty and activity of God in human affairs.

Perhaps the best way in is to read a full Gospel in one sitting. Mark will take less than an hour. You may never do it again, but it will give you an unforgettable sweep of the life of Jesus. You might do the same with a letter, say Philippians. So often we read a few verses of this or that book, and fail to grasp the whole message. Try also Genesis 1—12 for the 'true myths' which set the scene, the story of David from 1 Samuel 16 onwards for a picture of the archetypal king, Psalms 1–25 for an idea of the honesty and beauty of Jewish poetry and prayer, Isaiah 40—55 for a glimpse of the power of the prophetic writings, Acts for the amazing story of the early church. And always, but always, return to the Gospels and the theological portraits of Jesus.

Remember, the Bible is rather like the debris left over after an extraordinary explosion. What matters is not the precise configuration of the debris but what caused the explosion.

Levels of reading

The Bible can be read at all sorts of levels for different purposes, but consider three.

1 **For the Story.** The Story and stories of the Bible are at the heart of

our faith and our culture. Yet it is easy to make the assumption that they are known when in fact a generation of people is coming through with very little basic knowledge of them. We need to be a people of the Book, steeped in the Story, formed and shaped by it. So we need to read the Bible at this level to make sure that we can go on telling the Story in our culture.

2 **For study.** We can read the Bible to learn more of the ways of God and his people using all the tools of study and analysis, ranging from basic Bible reading notes to mighty commentaries. Here we open up the whole fascinating world of biblical studies, a pursuit which should inform the mind and, hopefully, also touch the heart.

3 **For transformation.** We can read the Bible in small amounts, intent not so much on greater understanding but on personal change. This may be because we use it to pray with, to meditate on, or to motivate action. The primary intention is to read it with the heart more rather than with the mind, although the two should never be out of touch with each other.

The methods of Bible reading which follow will relate to one or more of these levels. The variety means that different people can experiment with different methods because they are made differently! None is better (in spite of what we might think); they simply represent the variety of ways God meets and feeds his people through his word.

Bible-reading notes

This is the safest place to start for many people. It means that we are in the hands of thoughtful Christians who know their Bible, and have produced a coherent scheme of Bible study to help feed today's Christians. Notes are produced for three-month periods by, among others:

✳ Bible Reading Fellowship, Peter's Way, Sandy Lane West, Oxford OX4 5HG.

✳ *Every Day With Jesus*, Crusade for World Revival (CWR), Waverley Abbey House, Waverley Lane, Farnham, GU9 8EP.

✳ Scripture Union, 207 Queensway, Bletchley, Milton Keynes MK2 2EB.

Each organization produces a variety of notes for different kinds of users: for example young people, women, new Christians, as well as those who prefer concepts and ideas and those who do not. The best thing is to try the different styles to find what suits you, and not to be afraid of changing if and when you need. All these sets of notes will be available from a Christian bookshop.

Each set of notes gives suggestions for using them, but they work broadly along the following lines:

✳ **Pray:** ask for the wisdom and guidance of the Holy Spirit.

✳ **Read:** the passage designated, slowly, and twice if necessary.

✳ **Think:** what are your immediate responses, questions, thoughts?

✳ **Read the notes:** see what the writer has said in reflecting on the word (and don't worry if the notes are off-beam for you on a particular day. The Bible is rich enough to have many messages for different people at different times.).

✳ **Think again:** what does all this mean for me now in the way of new understanding or new action?

✳ **Pray:** out of all the above, for as long as you want or need, and in whatever way is right for you.

One thing to remember is that Bible-reading notes for every day can easily induce guilt! For very good reasons, we can easily miss a day or two, or more. And then the gap widens and the guilt grows. The danger then is to think that you are so hopeless at disciplined Bible reading that you might as well give it up altogether. A better response is either to re-engage with the notes at today's date and not be too legalistic, or alternatively to treat the notes as undated, and to go through them in your own time.

Bible reading without notes

It has to be admitted that some people just do not get on with Bible-reading notes. Either the comments irritate them, or they do not like being told how much to read, and on what day. On the other hand, they want to grapple seriously with God's word and to have it as a daily diet.

One answer is to read the Bible without notes but with a simple process of reflection and prayer, such as:

✶ **Pray:** ask for the wisdom and guidance of the Holy Spirit.

✶ **Read:** make your own choice about which book, Gospel or letter to read. It is important not to let your freedom become licence, and to wander around the Bible without purpose. Take a whole letter (e.g. 1 Corinthians) or a whole book (e.g. Nehemiah) or a section of a Gospel (e.g. the Sermon on the Mount, Matthew 5—7), and go through it at your own pace. It is well to note your own prejudices, for example against the Old Testament(!) and to make sure you have a balanced diet.

✶ **Think:** the important questions to consider are these:

  – What did this passage mean when it was originally written?
  – What does it mean today?
  – What should I do as a result?

You may find that a straightforward commentary is good to have beside you at this point, for example *The Bible Speaks Today* series from Inter-Varsity Press. For others who are not of the 'thinking' personality type, this would be anything but helpful!

✶ **Pray:** in your own way, but out of the passage and the reflections it has generated.

The Benedictine method

Background

This method will appeal to those who prefer to read the Bible in short sections in order to 'chew the word' and draw the sustenance out of it. Long passages of scripture, or Bible-reading notes generally, are too prescriptive and head-orientated for such people. The Benedictine method is ascribed to the sixth-century monk St Benedict because he took up and refined its use, establishing it as a widely used form of Bible-reading-and-prayer ever since. It is a reliable, standard method to return to if other methods of Bible reading go stale or you want a break. All you need is a Bible and the following steps.

Method

The approach is very simple and based on three words:

* **Reading** (*lectio*).

* **Meditation** (*meditatio*).

* **Prayer** (*oratio*).

1 **Reading.** Take up the Bible and start reading the passage you have chosen. Read it slowly and attentively and see where your attention is caught by a word, a phrase or a sentence. It will probably only be a very short time before something puts its head above the parapet and invites further thought and prayer.

2 **Meditation.** Now begin to chew that phrase over, to suck the goodness contained in it like a sweet in the mouth, to turn it over in your mind and heart. This will mean repeating it, probably many times, as you look at it this way and that, inside out and back to front. Hopefully it will yield up its treasures. This may take a couple of minutes or much longer – it should not be rushed; you don't have to get anywhere or complete the passage. It is getting the goodness out of the word of God that matters.

2 **Prayer.** Now turn your meditation into prayer. It may be that one

53

thought of praise, self-understanding or longing for God, or the need of some other person, has become the focus of your meditation. Whatever it is, that is the thing to take to the Lord prayerfully for as long as it takes.

Example

Suppose I have chosen the passage at the start of Paul's letter to the Philippians.

> Grace and peace to you from God our Father and the Lord Jesus Christ. I thank my God every time I remember you. In all my prayers for all of you I always pray with joy because of your partnership in the gospel from the first day until now.

Suppose now that the first phrase that hits me is 'I thank my God every time I think of you'. You stop . . . 'every time' . . . 'I thank my God *every time*' . . . with all the problems of his young churches Paul thanked God every time he thought of them . . . do I thank God for my church? Or do I tend to think first of its problems . . . 'every time' . . . sometimes, surely; not *every time* . . . What would it do if I thanked God every time I thought of the church council meeting? . . . 'I thank my God every time I think of you' . . . 'I thank my God' . . . is that perhaps a reflection of God's attitude as he thinks of us? . . . Does he rejoice in us, and take pleasure in us just being us, his children? . . . That would really be quite liberating . . .

And so our meditation might go on. But eventually it would come to a point where I would need to take some of this into prayer

> 'Lord, thank you for Paul's lovely attitude to his awkward churches. It would be so good to think like that too. Give me grace to be thankful for all my fellow Christians as I think of them. And I do think of them now. I think of . . . and . . . who sometimes irritate me so much at worship committee meetings. Thank you for their faithfulness and for their acceptance of me – because I probably irritate them just as much . . .'

And so the prayer continues for as long as is necessary, before the **reading (*lectio*)** continues again, if there is time.

'In all my prayers for all of you I always pray with joy . . .' Oh no! Not joy as well!

The Ignatian method

Background

People whose spirituality is experienced predominantly through the senses, as well as many others, often find Ignatian meditation a helpful way of reading the Bible and encountering Christ. The heart of this approach is that we enter into a biblical story and experience it from within. It means engaging all our senses so that we smell the sea, feel the rough ground under our feet, hear the conversations and so on.

Many people of course, particularly those whose spirituality is more a 'thinking' one which engages first with the mind, will find this approach difficult because it is plainly not real. However, God has more than one route into our lives, and the mind is not the only one. To be concerned about *history* is very important in the Christian faith, but to be concerned about *mystery* is also important, and Ignatian meditation enables us to engage other more intuitive and sensory parts of our brain. As well as the approach of reason and logic, there is the approach of metaphor and imagination. Each has its place in the amazingly colourful palette which God provides for us.

It is important in this type of meditation that we do not try to drive it in one predetermined direction. Which of us can escape our instincts, hurts and prejudices? Nevertheless we need to allow God to use our imaginations as freely as possible and to lead us to an encounter with him which will refresh and motivate us.

If this approach does not appeal to us immediately it may be for very good reasons of personality type, theology or upbringing, but it may be worth persevering a little longer, for this is a way that has been treasured by untold numbers of people through the years and it has become very popular again in recent years.

Again it may not be a method of Bible reading and prayer which we employ every day, since it requires time, quiet and some emotional effort. Nevertheless it is a form some people will want to use regularly and others occasionally.

Example
Bartimaeus: Mark 10.46–52

Read the story, slowly and carefully, and then put the Bible down. Close your eyes and begin to see the event unfold through your inner eye.

Jesus is leaving the city and you are caught up in the crowd ... be aware of the crowd, the throng of bodies, pushing gently to keep up ... look at the people around you ... what do you see on their faces? what emotions? ... Be aware of how they are dressed, what sort of cloth ... and of the hard ground beneath your feet, and the heat of the sun ... Jericho is so hot ...

The crowd is bunching up ... it must have stopped ... Work your way through the crowd and get to the front ... What do you see? ... There's a man on the ground ... look at him ... blind, like so many, sitting at the roadside asking anyone for money ... but something else is going on here ... Look at the blind man ... What do you see? ... and look at his face, what do you see there? ... He's got Jesus to stop, but some men around him don't look too pleased ... What has gone on here? ... Look at them again, the blind man and those standing by him ... Now turn to look at Jesus ... this is the closest you've been ... What do you see in him? ... in his eyes? ...

The man is getting to his feet ... Jesus must have said something ... did you hear it? ... Now Jesus and the man are facing each other ... watch them ... be aware of the atmosphere, the expectation ... Jesus speaks: listen to that voice in the quiet that's fallen all around ... 'What do you want me to do for you?' ... Does he mean that? ... and how does the blind man respond? ... Listen to his voice, and where it's coming from inside him ... see the body language ...

Watch Jesus as he answers that simple request ... and watch what he does ... and how he does it ... and what the man does as realization dawns ... watch him ... How do you feel about all this? ... What's going on inside you?

Now you realize that Jesus has turned to you ... he looks at you, straight on ... How do you feel? ... What do you see in his face, his eyes? ... He asks you the same question: 'What do you want me to do for you?' ... How do you answer him? ... Take your time ... he's not rushing you and everyone else is focused on Bartimaeus ... What do you say? ... tell him what you want ... How does Jesus respond to that? ... listen to him; talk with him ... Will you trust him? ... this is a crucial moment ... don't rush ... just talk ...

The time has come to move on ... Jesus turns away to continue down the road, leaving you standing there ... full of it ... full of him ... So what now? Where will you go? ... Something very special has happened ...

Just be quiet now for a while and rest in the presence of God.

Bible study in groups

Many people find it hard to study the Bible on their own. This might be for a number of reasons: the difficulties of this rich but complex book, the problem of motivation, or perhaps the extrovert preference for doing things with others and being sparked by their responses. Bible study in groups can be immensely rewarding, as evidenced by the millions of Christians worldwide who are involved in such study every week. The contexts are hugely varied: a Christian Union group at college, a 'base community' in South America, a church house group in suburban Britain, a group of catechists training in an African village – but all of them know that here in the King of Books they will be nourished in faith and hope, and above all, that here they are being dealt with by God himself.

The 'classic' Western method

The traditional approach to group Bible study in Western Europe and North America has stood the test of time. What it lacks in educational sophistication it gains in simplicity. Although there has recently been a demand for greater variety in Bible study method, this approach is a solid starting-point and place of return.

* Choose the passage carefully. This could happen in a number of ways:

- Work through a book, or parts of it: for example Acts, Ephesians, the Beatitudes in Matthew, a selection of Psalms.

- Use a published course from, for example, Bible Society, Church Pastoral Aid Society.

- Use the Common Lectionary readings for the following Sunday in church; it means people engage with the sermon much more closely!

- Select a series of topics of contemporary importance (work, leisure, debt) and choose one or more key Bible passages to dig into on each occasion.

- Let group members choose their own passage and lead the study on it.

* The passage is read aloud by one or more members of the group.

* Leader introduces the passage with background material he or she has gained in preparation through course notes and background books.

* Leader divides the passage up into manageable sections and introduces questions for discussion on each section.

* Leader sums up and leads into a time of prayer on issues that have come out of the discussion.

This method puts a lot of responsibility on the group leader. He or she must:

* have done a lot of preparation;

* have good judgement on the kinds of questions and issues which will fire the group;

* be aware of the factors which make or break groups and be able to handle them;

* have sufficient self-awareness to be able to control and critique people's prejudices and incipient megalomania!

The 'African' method

The African method is so called because it seems to be more common in parts of Africa.

This is a structured approach which requires a degree of commitment to the method as well as the content. The advantage is that it draws out of group members a deeper level of personal engagement with the text and its meaning.

* The group listens to *the passage being read aloud*. Silence is kept for reflection, to let the Word of God sink in.

* Each member of the group repeats aloud the word or phrase which particularly caught their attention. No comments are made at this point. We are gathering first points of impact.

* The passage is *read aloud a second time*, possibly by someone of the opposite gender from last time in order to change the way it is heard.

* Each member of the group is now invited to share their thoughts and insights from their hearing and thinking about the text. This leads into open discussion.

* Prayer and intercession is allowed to flow out of the discussion.

✳ The passage is now *read aloud for a third and last time* in order that the session is returned to the seminal Word of scripture.

The learning cycle

This approach builds on the strength of the well-known learning cycle used in many disciplines and many parts of the world. In particular it is a basic approach used in parts of South America where Christians come together not just for personal growth but also in order to plan for serious social change. Similar work was done in England by John Davies and John Vincent and it is their version of the learning cycle which we use here. It is, however, an approach which can just as well be used in an ordinary local church context because it picks up some crucial insights about how we learn and change through exposure to the Bible:

✳ We learn best if we start where we are, with our concerns and issues – like the first readers of the Gospels.

✳ The Gospels are subversive; they have a habit of catching us off-guard, of seeing things from a different angle, and so stimulating us to change.

✳ Everyone is able to teach us something unique about the Bible. We are all interpreters with something special to offer.

This is how the method works.

✳ **Story.** Listen to the story being read aloud and try to hear it afresh, as a story, without the accretions of the centuries or the embellishments of your own experience. (But how difficult it is to hear the Good Samaritan afresh!)

✳ **Snaps.** See where the story 'snaps' with your own experience, where it makes an immediate connection, and share that in the group. What does it remind you of, in any part of your life or memory? What contemporary issue in society does it bring to mind? What feelings does it arouse in you?

✳ **Study.** This is where the more serious thinking, the analysis, the theology, the more objective work, goes on. It may be that one member of the group has been asked to do the background reading on the history, religion, politics and social customs of the time, and to see what scholars have thought. But this only comes in now, after each member of the group has been able to identify with the text on their own terms. A period of discussion then ensues and goes on for as long as is necessary to unpack the text.

✻ **Spin-offs.** The next phase of the process is to ask in the group what are the spin-offs; what implications does all this have for us personally, for the church and its programme, for society – and what are we going to do about it? The focus turns back from the past on to the present and the seriousness of our engagement with the gospel. Have we been involved in a pleasant discussion or do we intend to respond to the gospel mandates with some action – possibly uncomfortable action?

The consequence of following this process is ideally that we start to write our own gospel events – a kind of 'fifth gospel' enacted in the life of the church today.

The Swedish Bible study method

The Swedish Bible study method is so called because it originated in that country.

Bible study can easily seem a very cerebral activity, to be all words and concepts. It can also seem to be something which goes on 'out there' rather than something which gets under the skin. The well-known Bible study method which follows attempts to engage each individual member of the group in their own questioning of the text. The discussion which ensues ought to be more personal and committed because of the individual work done first.

It is best to have photocopies of the text to be studied so that marks can be made on it as you go along.

✻ The passage is first read aloud.

✻ Everyone is then invited to go through their copy of the text marking it with the following symbols:

- Star: against anything which you think is particularly important.

- Question-mark: against anything which you do not understand.

- Light-bulb: against anything which strikes you afresh or sheds new light.

- Cross: against anything which seems offensive or wrong.

✳ The group then takes each symbol and discusses what members have marked with that symbol and why. Discussion can flourish at any point but is particularly likely to intensify around the question-marks and the crosses. This should not get out of balance with the positive messages of the stars and light-bulbs!

✳ A good leaving question is this: 'What will any of us do differently as a result of this Bible study?'

Participatory Bible study

For groups with some spark of adventure there is a whole range of different approaches to Bible study which are broadly called 'participatory'. They require more of a group member than the ability to sit in a chair and think for an hour and a half; they ask for active involvement. They also have the potential to bring a passage alive in a way which group members have never experienced before. Here we will consider just two examples, with further resources to be found in the 'Further Reading' chapter.

Character study

✳ A passage is chosen, such as the healing of the man in the tombs (Mark 5.1–20), and read clearly for the first time.

✳ The group divides into four sub-groups, representing the demon-possessed man, the disciples, the herdsmen, and the local people. The groups sit together in different corners. They are told they have to listen to the story again, but this time to hear it as the character they represent in their sub-group.

✳ The passage is read again.

✳ The sub-groups/'characters' have 15 minutes to think out together how they feel about the story and the part they have had in it, and what questions they would like to put, or what they would like to say, to the other 'characters'. There are grounds in this story for a fair amount of anger, confusion, puzzlement and defensiveness. How will the disciples justify their master's actions which have destroyed the economic prosperity of a large number of local people? How does the healed man feel about being left behind to face the prejudice and anger of the people?

✳ The 'characters' now get together and begin the discussion. The leader has to orchestrate the questioning of each character by the others and the ensuing exchanges. Ideally the characters should speak in their own character. For example: 'We herdsmen are feeling pretty angry with you foreigners. You just come over here, cool as you like, and send our livelihood into the sea to drown! So are you going to pay us compensation or what?'

✳ After a 'full and frank exchange of views' the leader begins to draw out the contemporary parallels. Who do we scapegoat in our society, and how do we react to their rescue when, for example, huge resources are poured into their needs? How should we evaluate the respective worth of human beings and animals in, for example, animal experiments for medical purposes?

Fresh insights are almost guaranteed!

Biblical modelling

It should not be thought that just because this method involves a degree of dramatic display that older people will not warm to it. Just watch them! The method is simple but the insights can be profound, and the risks are actually minimal.

✳ An incident is taken such as the miracle of Jesus turning water into wine (John 2.1–11). The passage is read clearly and well.

✳ The group is divided up into characters: Jesus, the disciples, Mary his mother, the bride, the groom, the steward, the disciples, the servants. If there are not enough people, economize on the bride (!) and the disciples.

✳ The passage is read a second time so that this time the group members hear it through the ears of their own character.

✳ The group now has to create a freeze-frame picture of what it could have looked like at the wedding reception after the water had been found to be high-quality wine. How would the body language of the characters express their thoughts and feelings? To prepare this scene the characters have got to talk to each other to try to work out what the likely effect really was on each of the characters. It is this discussion which forms the basis of the Bible study.

✳ The freeze-frame is then enacted. Each person in turn can be invited to leave the scene for a minute and walk around it, looking at the way each person is represented.

* Afterwards, further discussion can follow, ending with the question: 'What do you now understand differently about this incident and had not realized before?'

A variation on this is to take a scene with fewer characters and to have a number of sub-groups working on it at the same time. Each group then presents their freeze-frame of the scene, and discussion follows on the different perceptions of the various groups about what was really going on. Possible subjects include:

* The Prodigal Son – father, two sons (Luke 15.11–32).

* Mary and Martha – Jesus (or the disciples), Mary, Martha (Luke 10.38–42).

* The Last Supper – Jesus, Peter, John, Judas (John 13.21–30 and Luke 22.31–34).

They said that

'We present you with this Book, the most valuable thing that this world affords. Here is wisdom; this is the royal Law. These are the lively oracles of God.'
WORDS SPOKEN ON PRESENTING THE BIBLE TO THE SOVEREIGN AT A CORONATION

The Bible is alive, it speaks to me; it has feet, it runs after me; it has hands, it lays hold on me.   MARTIN LUTHER

When we come to the Bible, we come to be changed, not to amass information.   RICHARD FOSTER

It had been one of my fears that reciting the Gospel might be a dull exercise; that I would have to manufacture energy. Now I had new fears. I was afraid that I wouldn't have the energy to sustain it. I was afraid that I wouldn't be able to keep up with Mark's pace. I was afraid that the speed of Mark's reporting might defeat me. But I was also thrilled beyond measure. This was the greatest script I had ever found.
ACTOR ALEC MCCOWAN, ON HIS ONE-MAN PRESENTATION OF MARK'S GOSPEL

'No Bible, no breakfast!'   THE REVD H. LEA, FORMER RECTOR OF EDGWARE

[I agreed to translate the gospels for Penguin books.] My personal reason for doing this was my intense desire to satisfy myself as to the authority and spiritual content of the gospels. My work changed me. I came to the conclusion that these words bear the seal of the Son of Man and the Son of God. And they're the Magna Carta of the human spirit.   DR E. V. RIEU

Most people are bothered by those passages of Scripture which they cannot understand. But as for me, I always notice that the passages of Scripture which trouble me most, are those that I *do* understand.
MARK TWAIN

Voltaire said, 'One hundred years from my death, the Bible will be a museum piece.' A hundred years later the French Bible Society set up their new headquarters in Voltaire's old home in Paris.
SOURCE UNKNOWN

The Bible is food for wrestlers.   D. T. NILES

4 Beginning again with the church

Belonging

For many Christians belonging to Christ is one thing; belonging to the church is another. For this is where the going gets hard. This is where otherwise sane people become obsessive about flower stands, extraordinarily daft things are said from pulpits, music seems to come from Hymns A and M (ancient and morbid), and people's rich, warm personalities are taken off and left at the door.

Nevertheless, these are the wonderful, infuriating, Godly, eccentric, gifted people whom God has given us as our companions on the journey, and whether we can cope with them and love them is one of the acid tests of our discipleship. We belong to each other in a way no secular group or society comes close even to understanding, for we are all members of the holy body of Christ. We can no more rid ourselves of our brothers and sisters in Christ and remain Christian, than we can rid ourselves of Christ himself. We are, in fact, a community of the friends of Jesus and therefore we accept and enjoy each other as those who have that Friend in common.

Another biblical image of the local church is that it is made up of bricks which together are built into a spiritual house (1 Peter 2.5). It matters less what each brick achieves than that it is there, doing the job it has to do. Each of us matters uniquely in the house of God's people and without us the house is incomplete. This may strike us as surprising when we think of some of our 'fellow bricks' who seem to us to be awkward and sharp-edged and designed for an alternative career in the house of God down the road, but we have to resist the urge to help them on their way! We are all of ultimate and infinite value to the Lord of the house.

Even if we get to the point of near hysteria and would prefer to watch the omnibus edition of *Neighbours* than go to church, we should beware the temptation to wander off and try to find a perfect church. If you find one, don't join it, because you will wreck it! A perfect church needs perfect Christians, and there aren't any.

God has graciously given us a huge variety of ways of worshipping him, and the first church we go to may simply not be offering the kind of worship and church life which is most conducive to our own spiritual growth and therefore our ability to serve others. This is a difficult point.

On the one hand, there is a sensible presumption that we should worship in our local church in our own locality. This is where we can worship with our neighbours, bear our Christian witness naturally amongst them, and serve our community in the name of Christ. The presumption of the New Testament church was that people worshipped locally, as also has been the presumption of the church through the ages. Moreover, it seems to be the case today that what is local is real.

On the other hand, increased mobility has changed many social patterns, and people are used to going to the bank, supermarket and lesiure centre that they like. Moreover the varieties of expression of worship and church life correspond to varieties of human personality. Different people will find different settings more congenial than others and therefore more helpful to their spiritual journey.

Perhaps we should retain the presumption in favour of the local church but be prepared to look further if it is really necessary. We need a place where we are broadly comfortable with the traditions and ways of the church – and then stick with it through thick and thin. 'Church-hopping' is rarely good for anyone's spiritual health. There is always a natural inclination to go where the fire is burning brightly and giving off real warmth. But if we all go to the 'in' place, what happens to the need for Christian presence and witness in other communities where the fire is burning low? Christians need to go where the fire needs fanning as well as where the flames are high.

We should also be prepared to experiment to find which of the services of that church is the right one for us. A quiet early communion or a busy family serivce? A dignified eucharist or a swinging-from-the-rafters praise service? A meditative Taizé evening or cathedral evensong? The good news is that Jesus is the same, yesterday, today and for ever – and in each of these services that call upon his name.

A key distinction to make is that between expectation and expectancy. Our expectations of the church should be high but realistic. Every church is a gathering of the walking wounded, some doing better than others but all of us damaged in one way or another. This is what makes churches potentially such places of healing. The church is a laboratory of the human, the place where we find out and experiment with the glorious task of becoming fully human and fully alive – ransomed, healed, restored and forgiven. But there will be disappointments along the way and we must not throw out the baby of faith with the dirty bath water of the church.

It may help to think of a room where young children have been playing all day. When we go in after they have gone to have their tea the room looks like a disaster area. Toys and games lie everywhere, scattered around chaotically. What we may be conscious of is simply a mess. There is no life in these discarded objects lying knee-deep across the floor. However, when the children come back after tea and begin playing again, the whole situation changes. Life returns. The chaos becomes meaningful; the mess is actually an arena of purpose and pleasure for the children and their parents. Similarly, the church, when viewed by an outsider, may appear a mess. This is the way it is sometimes portrayed in the media. All that appears is muddle and confusion – lifeless objects covering the floor. However, when you see in the midst of the mess the presence of Christ, it all begins to make sense. This is the arena of divine play, of the rich and colourful life of God, poured out for us in reckless love. In response to that love we play the best we can, and try to keep hitting each other to a minimum! But what was formerly unintelligible, now becomes marvellously alive. Our expectations of the church therefore have to be high, but realistic enough to recognize that it often appears to be a bit of a mixed bag, both to us and to others.

Expectancy, on the other hand, can never be high enough. When we come to church to worship, we are coming to meet with God. Worship is the technicolour film of our faith. It is offering all of ourselves to all God has revealed himself to be, and the outcome should be change. The result of truly encountering the terror and beauty of God is not conformity but transformation. We are broken open to the invasion of the Spirit, to the mystery of each other, and to the wounds of the world. When we come to worship we don't come to twiddle our thumbs. Expectancy is fully justified because it is directed towards God's activity and not ours. He can be trusted to be present and active. A South American Christian had once been travelling in England and was asked on his return what he thought of the worship. 'The services always start on time,' he said, 'even if the Holy Spirit hasn't turned up yet!' Our expectancy must be directed towards God.

That, at least, is the theory. What it requires of us is a holy expectancy which then becomes a holy obedience to the will and the wonder of God. But we have to look with expectancy. We have to listen until our ears pop. We have to strain our spirits for the word and the touch of Christ, which may come in the most unexpected ways. It may be a phrase of a Bible reading that quickens our pulse; it may be a verse of a hymn that has never touched us like that before; it may be an idea in a sermon, not even intended, but a throwaway, lying at the side of the path; it may be the act of receiving communion which suddenly floods the heart with delight, or the smile on the face of a child, or a shaft of sunlight through stained-glass windows. Who knows how God will choose to break into our life and steal our heart away? The point is to be ready for it, to be looking, listening and longing. To be expectant.

Praying the service

The danger in a leisure-soaked society is that people come to church to be entertained. They would never say that of course, but we have grown so used to an entertainment industry which delivers very high standards of technical and professional presentation that our attempts to worship God on a Sunday morning get put unconsciously into the same bracket of leisure provision that we see on television and elsewhere. And the church comes out rather badly. The choir is out of tune, the overhead projector is crooked, the minister loses his place, the lesson-reader obviously doesn't have a clue what's going on in his bit of the Old Testament, and generally the service seems to be on the verge of a nervous breakdown.

One answer to this is to tell ourselves very clearly that we are not here for Christian entertainment; we are here to pray, and our contribution to the service is by praying through it, and that is every bit as important as what is going on out at the front.

* **Praying before the service.** I cannot verify this, but I suspect that when some people come into a church, slip into a pew and kneel down for a few moments, what they actually do is count to ten, and when it seems that a respectable time has elapsed, they get up again. This may be a libel! However, we can at least make sure that before the service we really pray for those leading the service, for the children's work and their leaders, for any newcomers to church, and for ourselves, that we should truly meet God.

* **Praying the hyms and songs.** It is very easy to sing hymns without having a clue what it is we are singing about. It requires a conscious effort to think about the words and to sing them from the inside, but the effect is enormously beneficial. Our hymns contain some wonderful expressions of Christian truth, great poetry, stirring themes, evocative ideas, exciting promises, and deep reassurance. Even one verse, properly sung, can give us enough food to chew on for the rest of the service.

✳ **Listen prayerfully to the Word.** When the Bible is read to us we are not hearing someone's useful thoughts or listening to the wisdom of a few good men. We are encountering the living Word of God, and our job is not to stand over it (in judgement) but to stand under it (in obedience). The act of sitting down when the reading starts sometimes seems as if it is a signal to disengage the brain and let the mind wander off to who's in church this morning, how this afternoon's televised football match will go, and when to fill in that annoying tax form. Listening is an active commitment. It takes effort and concentration, but the rewards are infinite, for here we are being addressed by God himself. What did this passage mean when it was written? What does it say to me now? Pray for understanding before, during and after the reading.

✳ **Pray the prayers.** That sounds fairly obvious but the point needs to be made. We may be conscious of many things about the prayers and the person leading them, and not in fact get round to praying them ourselves. The sugary tone of voice may put us off, or the strange choice of words, or the interminable length. We may wonder why this was prayed for and not that, and did we really have to have that same old list of the same old places where we pray the same old prayers for the same old things – not really expecting God to do anything about it? The alternative is that we enter the prayers with hunger and commitment; these are people and places in real need of the touch and activity of our loving God. We can truly lift these people to him, bear the weight of their pain, and love them enough to be serious in our praying. The spoken prayers from the front are just springboards for the prayer of our own hearts. That is what God can use.

✳ **Pray for the preacher.** As with the readings, there can be a similar reaction of closing down the mind when the preacher climbs into the pulpit. Years of sermons, many not particularly memorable, have inoculated many churchgoers against the importance of the sermon. But here is a privilege and responsibility before which men and women should tremble. The great responsibility of the preacher is to interpret the eternal Word of God into the current experience of this church and culture. Anyone who has that task needs praying for! Our part therefore is to pray for the preacher, as he or she starts; to pray for all of us in the congregation, that we should be open to the personal word of the Lord to us; and to pray that the Holy Spirit will be the interpreter in our midst. And if the preacher seems to be losing it, pray even harder!

* **Pray the communion.** If the service is one of Holy Communion, there are other places to focus our prayer. The most important one is the act of receiving the bread and wine itself. As we go up to receive communion our minds can be full of many things: Are my clothes straight? Are people looking at me? Can I avoid tripping up at the step? When shall I go forward to the rail? And so on. This is probably inevitable, but at least we can be sure as we wait for our time to go up that we are opening ourselves actively to God, praying for his touch, taking to him our concerns. Then when we actually get to receive the bread and wine, we can intend, in the holding open of our hands, to bring to God all our problems, dilemmas and decisions, together with the emptiness of our hearts, so that they may be filled with the goodness and life of Christ himself. And the only response possible when we have taken the bread and wine into ourselves is to say – thank you, thank you.

* **Praying the end.** That is not the same as praying *for* the end! It means that when the service ends we do not leap up looking for the first person whom we need to talk to over coffee. It means we can stay in our seat, recalling the gifts God has given us in the service, the insights, the encouragement, the moments of pleasure, and thank him for them. We can pledge ourselves to take Sunday out into Monday, and to live our worship in our daily lives. And we can pray for anyone of whom we have become particularly conscious in the service, and who might appreciate a chat now.

All in all, the ordinary morning service can become quite an adventure of prayer.

Understanding Holy Communion

Whether Holy Communion is celebrated rarely or often, and whether it is called the eucharist, the mass or the Lord's supper, theologians of all traditions agree that this service is the heart of Christian worship. This is what Jesus told his infant church to do – to 'do this' in remembrance of him. And ever since, the church has known Christ in the breaking of bread and the sharing of wine, an action utterly characteristic of the church on any continent, at any period, for almost any reason. Wherever there has been something significant to mark, most Christians have found no better thing to do – not least in the steady passage of the church's life – as the people of God have met together to be remade and renewed.

The problem, however, is how to understand the mystery at the heart of the service, and much blood and ink has been spilt through the centuries as people have struggled to interpret the inner reality of communion. Many much wiser attempts have been made to describe some of the elements of the service simply, but I offer here a straightforward acrostic, based on the fact that at the centre of the meaning of the service, on any understanding, is the cross of Jesus Christ. We might therefore grasp some of the dimensions of communion in this way:

Community

Remembrance

Offering

Spirit

Service

* **Community.** Holy Communion is the festive meal of the family of God. It is not merely a personal encounter between the individual believer and his or her God. It is the meal which shapes and forms a people, just as family meals – or the absence of them these days – shapes and holds a human family together. By gathering around a table – the Lord's table – we are bound to be drawn into human contact with all those who are similarly gathered, and a community is born. Paul was particularly concerned to hear that in the church in Corinth people were coming to the Lord's supper and getting into groups with their friends and ignoring the needs of their poorer fellow Christians who had come straight up from work in the docks, and had not got any food for tea. He warned them that they had to 'recognize the body of the Lord' or they would be bringing themselves under judgement (1 Corinthians 11.28). Communion implies community.

* **Remembrance.** This is an interesting word. It is not the same as

remembering. The latter is the act of calling to mind a past event. Remembrance, on the other hand, is about 'standing inside' and re-owning the event, as for example in the annual Remembrance Day ceremonies all over Britain. When you stand on Hadrian's wall and feel the fear of the lonely Roman soldier at night in a barbarian land; when you stand on the battlefield at Waterloo and imagine the Imperial Guard making their last doomed assault up the hill, then you are getting in touch with remembrance. Remembrance makes a past event present in the mind and heart of the individual and the community. In Holy Communion, therefore, it is the cross and resurrection which become vivid realities for the believer, who exeriences again their centrality and power. The cross is where the great battle was fought and Christ overcame the forces of evil on their own ground, for us and for all people. The resurrection is where the power of the new Christ flooded into the world to make free and authentic living a possibility for everyone. In Holy Communion, all of this is focused in broken bread and shared wine. Past and present fuse in a single reality, and Christ makes his presence available to us again, through his Spirit, in that bread and wine.

* **Offering.** This is another concept much fought over in Christian history. However, it is possible simply to recognize that somewhere near the heart of this service is a transaction. We bring our lives to God; Christ gives his life to us. Here is a mutual offering. When we approach the taking of bread and wine, we come with hands that are both full and empty. They are *full* of the burdens and delights of our last week, of things to be thankful for and things to disturb our peace. We may bring to him our family, our work, our plans, the week ahead. We offer all this to God, for him to take and transform, to use and to shape, and to give back to us as we are able to receive it, through the week. At the same time our hands are *empty* because there is nothing of our own that we can bring that is able to earn us a place in God's kingdom; we are honest pilgrims needing the grace and gifts of Jesus Christ, above all the gift of his own life in ours, 'bubbling up to eternal life' (John 4.14). Christ, in his humility, gives himself to us, so that 'we are in him and he is in us'. What we experience therefore is the mutual offering of Christ and the believer, in a union of love.

* **Spirit.** We have thought so far about Holy Communion as an encounter with God focused on the cross and resurrection of Jesus.

But communion is just as much about the work of the Holy Spirit. It is the Spirit who draws together the disparate people of God into a holy family. It is the Spirit who makes real the critical events of Jesus' life, and his presence in our midst now. It is the Spirit who acts as the go-between for Christ and his people in mutual self-offering. The service of Communion therefore is suffused with the presence and work of the Spirit, and we should recognize the Spirit of God hovering over the whole process and making the communion holy. Ultimately what the Spirit is doing is giving us a foretaste of the heavenly banquet when all God's people will be gathered with him in praise and delight. For now, the *holy community* gathers to receive *holy communion* as a foretaste of the *holy kingdom* which God intends for us all.

✳ **Service.** At the end of the Anglican Communion service is the dismissal: 'Go in peace to love and serve the Lord.' The end result of any communion should be that the Lord's people are strengthened for service in the world. People should be changed by the eucharist. As Michael Ramsey, former Archbishop of Canterbury, once said: 'The question is not, what do we make of the Eucharist, but what is the Eucharist making of us.' To raise the stakes a bit, Communion ought to have a Spiritual Health Warning which should say: 'Warning, this service will change you.' If we are not, inch by painful inch, being transformed by Christ in Communion, then there must be some blockage in the system. As a parishioner once said to me, searching hard for the right words, 'That Communion service . . . it's a ball of fire.'

Communion gives us our battle rations as Christians. Or, if that is too militaristic an image, it provides us with the food of the fools of Christ. Either way, as soldiers or as fools, it is what we go out to do in the rest of our lives that really counts. The reality of faith is found in the thousand details of our lives, from the way we spend our time to the way we spend our money; from the way we love our families to the way we love our unloveable neighbour. Faith is always tested in action, and communion gives us the best possible resources of strength and inspiration to carry on the patient service of Christ to his broken world.

Writing many years ago, Gregory Dix reflected on the command of Jesus to 'do this in remembrance of me':

Was ever command so obeyed? For century after century, spreading slowly to every continent and country and among every race on earth, this action has been done in every conceivable human circumstance. Men have found no better thing than this to do for kings at their crowning and for criminals going to the scaffold; for armies in triumph or for a bride and a bridegroom in a little country church; for the wisdom of the Parliament of a mighty nation or for a sick old woman afraid to die; for a schoolboy sitting an exam or for Columbus setting out to discover America; in thankfulness because my father did not die of pneumonia; because the Turk was at the gates of Vienna; for the settlement of a strike; for Captain So-and-So, wounded and a prisoner of war; while the lions roared in a nearby amphitheatre; on the beach at Dunkirk; tremulously by an old monk on the fiftieth anniversary of his vows; furtively, by an exiled bishop who has hewn timber all day in a prison camp near Murmansk; georgeously for the canonization of St Joan of Arc – one could fill many pages with the reasons men have done this and not tell a hundredth part of them. And best of all, week by week and month by month, on a hundred thousand successive Sundays, across all the parishes of Christendom, the pastors have 'done this' just to *make* the holy common people of God.

Gregory Dix, *The Shape of the Liturgy*, Dacre Press, 1945

What's it all for anyway?

So far we have been thinking about belonging to a church and how to make the most of its worship. Behind the shop window, however, is a much bigger question. What is the church for anyway? Why all the paraphernalia of church organization? Why could we not just get on with loving God and our neighbour and leave it at that? Oh that life were so simple! For the same reason that we use money rather than bartering, live in houses rather than caves, and use telephones and e-mail rather than messengers on horseback, the church has had to have a structure in order to carry out Jesus' command to take the gospel to the whole world.

But what exactly is the mission of the church in a complex world 2,000 years after Jesus gave us that command? How do we translate the profound simplicities of the gospel of Jesus Christ into our contemporary setting? One of the best statements we have at present came out of the Anglican

Consultative Council in 1990 and has been gaining recognition more widely ever since. It says this:

The work of the Church is the mission of Christ:

* to proclaim the good news of the Kingdom

* to teach, baptize and nurture new believers

* to respond to human need by loving service

* to seek to transform the unjust structures of society

* to strive to safeguard the integrity of creation, and sustain and renew the life of the earth.

To proclaim the Good News of the kingdom

There is no substitute for the basic proclamation of the fact that Jesus came with love from the Father, and showed us the possibilities of being a full human being; that he died for our sins, was buried and on the third day rose again; and that the kingdom of God has broken in decisively in this life-death-resurrection of Jesus. The message that Jesus has come, with forgiveness, to bring us life in all its fullness, needs to be offered and proclaimed in season and out of season. It needs to be done in a thousand million ways, for each Christian has his or her own story to tell of the gracious action of God in their own life, and that story is the window into God's story for the people we meet and talk to.

What is my part in this?

* Think about your own story. Perhaps use the diagram of the journey in section 1 of this book to clarify your mind. What are the main steps by which you have come to faith? What difference has it made?

* Be prepared to tell your story, or parts of it, to people who express an interest. Tell it graciously and courteously, as God has dealt with you.

* Resolve never to let your life contradict your message!

To teach, baptize and nurture new believers

The church has a story, God's story, which it has to tell. It also has a community life of prayer, fellowship and service into which the new believer is brought and nurtured. The process is one of being 'incorporated' into

Christ, built into his body. The teaching work of the church is carried on in a huge number of ways, from home Bible study groups to university departments of theology, from Alpha courses to confirmation groups, from the writing of books (of which there is no end!) to retreat houses and prayer schools. Christians should never stop growing, for the very good reason that we have never done anything more than scratch the surface of the mystery of God.

What is my part in this?

* Be a 'companion on the way' for others. We all need friends to journey with us. Who do you recognize is starting on the journey of faith and might appreciate your companionship?

* Look for opportunities to deepen your understanding of the faith. It has been said that the average British Christian is as well equipped to meet an aggressive atheist as a boy with a pea-shooter is to meet a tank! But the resources are vast: books, courses, study days, retreats, workshops, conferences. Details from your minister, church magazine, church press, denominational headquarters, Christian bookshop etc.

* Consider offering to teach children or young people in church groups on Sundays or midweek. There is nothing like having to teach others for making us learn ourselves!

To respond to human need by loving service

We worship a God who washes feet. The inescapable mark of a follower of Jesus is that he or she will be committed to practical action and be prepared to love beyond the limits. It is not surprising that the contemporary icon of Christianity that the world recognized was Mother Teresa – a nun committed to working with the poorest of the poor dying on the streets of Calcutta. People rightly expect there to be a difference in the way we live. It may mean that our lives are under scrutiny, but that is fair enough. We are following a different way and claiming a different power. Some parishioners came to church one morning and found the door locked. Pinned on to the door, however, was a notice from the vicar: 'We've been coming here long enough. Now let's go and do it.' And we 'do it' in the details of our lives, by stopping to listen, by remembering to write that note, by staying on to clear up, by noticing who is being left out.

What is my part in this?

❋ Cultivate the art of looking under the surface and listening between the lines. That is where the needs will be found.

❋ When you meet someone, ask yourself what is likely to be their major concern or interest, not what you can get out of the meeting. It is simple care for others.

❋ Consider helping the church family in some straightforward but necessary way. Coffee rotas and church-cleaning lists are not glamorous areas of service, but they are nevertheless absolutely essential to the well-being of the church. I often think that God's little people are his favourites!

❋ Identify where a social need is most sharply felt in your area and offer your help – homelessness, a hospice, Victim Support, Samaritans. But remember that some periods of our lives may not allow this (early motherhood, for example), so don't feel guilty!

To seek to transform the unjust structures of society

Bishop Lesslie Newbigin once asked a group of church elders what their church was for. After a long silence, someone said that it was there to meet the needs of its members. 'Then,' said the bishop, 'it should be dissolved immediately.' We do not exist for ourselves, but for the world which God loved so much that he sent his only son (John 3.16). One theologian said that the kingdom of God is a healed creation. The stakes are high. What this means is that we are not concerned just to get people into church; our concern is to go out from the church to work for God's huge enterprise of renewing his world, taking his 'shalom' into every corner of creation. This may mean social and political action of a sacrificial nature: the church had many martyrs in the fight against apartheid in South Africa and against tyranny in Central America. Our vision of God and his purposes is never big enough.

What is my part in this?

❋ Every contribution matters in any great enterprise. Being a member of Amnesty, the World Development Movement, Friends of the Earth etc. is at least a statement of intent. Active involvement in a local group is even better.

* Be a committed supporter of Christian Aid or Tear Fund, or other aid agency, and consider helping to raise funds. When millions die every year from hunger and avoidable disease, there can be few more basic challenges than that of Jesus: 'I was hungry and you gave me something to eat.' (Matthew 25.35)

* Track your political commitment back to your faith. Make sure the two relate to one another. Ask moral questions about political policies.

* Buy fairly traded products and support companies with ethical investment policies.

To strive to safeguard the integrity of creation, and sustain and renew the life of the earth

The green agenda is not just a political fad; it is a part of the 'healed creation' of the previous section. It is an expression of the fundamental Christian conviction that God loved his world into existence and sustains it by that love. He has created untold diversity in the natural world as a reflection of the extraordinary richness of his own being. Creation, however, is a continuing act of exquisite balance and fragility, and our responsibility is to care for the earth which God entrusted to humankind as his stewards. Environmental issues have become critical and Christians should be in the forefront of those concerned to save the planet. We of all people have a mandate from the Maker whose instructions have not been well-enough followed.

What is my part in this?

* Be informed, and never let the environmental case be ignored.

* Think about joining Friends of the Earth or Greenpeace.

* Think globally and act locally: be committed to recycling, using the car less, and to as much simple living as possible.

Ten things to do in a boring sermon

1 **Forgive the preacher!** (unless she makes a habit of it). We don't know if she had a bad week, a blinding headache or simply ran out of inspiration. In any case, not all ministers are gifted in preaching. The bottom line is: 'As the Lord has forgiven you, so you also must forgive.' (Colossians 3.13)

2 **Resolve not to go for any cheap shots afterwards**, such as 'Well, you always manage to find something to fill up the time,' 'It's a shame they make you preach so often,' or 'Did you know there are 236 panes of glass in the east window?' Rise above this temptation.

3 **Pray for the preacher.** It can't do any harm. But don't be too optimistic either. Remember the vicar's daughter who asked her mother why daddy said a prayer before he preached. 'He asks God to help him,' came the answer. Pause. 'Then why doesn't God help him?' asked the little girl (on behalf of the congregation).

4 **Pray for the congregation.** This is actually very important because God can use almost anything to speak to people's hearts. A word, a phrase, a half-formed idea, even a misheard idea – all can take seed in a listener's mind. The proof of this divine cunning is the number of times a preacher is warmly thanked for something she is sure she never said!

5 **Think of a good line to help the preacher re-examine his preaching technique.** Try: 'Thank you for having a go at that subject today. But what really interests me about it is this . . .' In other words, get him to think harder about his preaching. If you really want to put the wind up him, you might even suggest setting up a group to discuss his sermon with him regularly. (But be prepared for a small attendance.)

6 **Pray for yourself**, for a forgiving spirit and a good lunch. Or more constructively, pray that God will give you that one pearl which makes the sludge worthwhile.

7 **Think how you might preach on this same passage.** What would be your main point? How would it relate to the congregation's current experience, and yours? How would you illustrate it? Can you think of a memorable phrase to sum it up so that people might go out 'humming the sermon' instead of the last hymn?

8 **Put the sermon in a broader context.** Remember there are hundreds of thousands of sermons being preached all over the world this morning, and some of them are going to be barnstormers. Briefly regret the fact that this is not one of them, but praise God for those people who are being challenged and changed even now in other luckier places.

9 **If you are having as bad a day as the preacher, allow yourself some extra-curricular activity.** A small survey in my home revealed the following favourites: count how many people nearby have dyed their hair; plan next week's menus (or next month's); find a small child and watch it for acts of spectacular freedom. Failing everything, start rattling your watch to see if it's broken.

10 **Pray for the Second Coming,** when all preaching will be unnecessary.

But here's one thing *not* to do: don't ever lower your sights in what you expect of the sermon. Here should be a divine–human exchange of the highest order. Remember the words of Thomas Carlyle: 'Who, having been called to be a preacher, would stoop to be a king?' Put that on your Christmas card to the vicar.

They said that

Christians come together in order to meet God in the company of each other, and to meet each other in the presence of God.   DAVID WATSON

God invites the whole of humanity to share in his exploration of a new world. The Church is simply those members of the expedition who know the one who is leading it.   JOHN V. TAYLOR

The East Harlem Sunday School was asked to describe the kind of people who came to church. 'Big people come to church,' said one. 'Children come to church,' said another. 'Fat people come to church,' said a third. 'Yes,' a small boy piped up, surely delighting his Maker's heart, 'and bad people come to church too.'   BRUCE KENDRICK

If you don't worship, you'll shrink; it's as brutal as that.
PETER SCHAFFER

Carl Jung had been counselling a man for six months but he was getting no better. Finally Jung said: 'Friend, I can do no more for you. What you need is God.' 'How do I find God, Dr Jung?' the man asked. 'I don't know,' said Jung, 'but I suspect if you find a group of people who believe in him passionately and just spend time with them, you will find God.' SOURCE UNKNOWN

The question to be asked about every congregation is not: how big is it? How fast is it growing? How rich is it? It is: what difference is it making to that bit of the world in which it is placed? Is it actually functioning as a first fruit, a sign and an instrument of God's new creation for that bit of the world? LESSLIE NEWBIGIN

To worship is to quicken the conscience by the holiness of God
        to feed the mind with the truth of God
        to purge the imagination by the beauty of God
        to open the heart to the love of God
        to devote the will to the purpose of God.
All this is gathered up in that emotion which most cleanses us from selfishness becuse it is the most selfless of all emotions – adoration.
WILLIAM TEMPLE

The Church of the future will not seek to control, but to transform and transfigure. The second Christendom will have more of the still small voice. It will express a quieter purpose within society, embodied in many individuals and groups, often small, healing, binding up, caring, creating new links. It will be a weaving of loving relationships, a quiet transforming of one family, one school, one work-place; a subtle all-pervading influence. In one word, a leaven. JOHN LAWRENCE

5 Beginning again with a Christian lifestyle

Singing the Lord's song in a strange land

The cultural context

Our culture is increasingly called a postmodern culture. Few people understand what that means! An article in the *Independent* newspaper said: 'This word has no meaning. Use it as often as possible.' Nevertheless one can say that a postmodern society:

✻ likes to pick 'n mix

✻ enjoys being laid back and playful

✻ distrusts logic, reason and the idea of progress

✻ is suspicious of tradition and authority

✻ likes fuzzy boundaries

✻ refuses to judge, and views all opinions with equal tolerance.

Critics of postmodernism would say that:

✻ a 'pick 'n mix' approach avoids anything difficult or disturbing

✻ babble replaces discussion and dialogue

✻ pools of ignorance replace accepted knowledge

✻ everything is allowable; if it feels good, do it

✻ opinion passes for truth; relativism rules.

Such a context presents Christians with a number of difficulties as well as a number of opportunities. In contrast to the 1960s and 1970s the Christian case can often find a hearing, because it is a world view held by a large number of people. On the other hand it will often not be allowed to make any final claim to truth since all world views are equally a matter of personal opinion. Christianity thus becomes another option in a world of alternatives.

There is a renewed emphasis therefore on the way that Christians live. The negative side of it is that the truth claims of Christianity don't matter, according to postmodernism; what matters is how it is lived. The positive side of it is that it asks proper questions of Christians and the integrity of their lifestyle, and it gives an opportunity for non-believers to be impressed by the difference that Christian faith can make. 'By their fruits you will know them.' (Matthew 7.16)

The freedoms and the limits of individualism

One crucial gain of postmodernism is that it helps us to have confidence in our uniqueness and individuality. The Christian faith does not come to us in a package, wrapped up like a sandwich from a motorway service area. It does not come as a complete set of beliefs and practices from which any variation will lead to disaster. It comes to us instead as a relationship which has to be worked out in the free-flowing grace of God's love for us and ours for him.

There are still versions of Christianity around that seem to depend more on law than on grace. They seem to impose a new legalism, a set of rules about what to believe, how to pray, how to spend weekday evenings, and maybe, what television programmes to watch. To step outside these regulations is to risk the disapproval of the community, a visit from the minister, and at least a few question-marks about your eternal destination! The reality, however, is that we are utterly unique in our make-up, our needs, our inner life, and therefore in the way God deals with us. Our spiritual journey and the way we live out our discipleship will be as unique as our fingerprints.

God has shown himself to be outrageously broad-minded in the people he has called and the way he has used them. Take, for example, St Simon sitting on a pillar for years, Martin Luther King leading the attack on racial discrimination in the United States, Rublev painting icons outside Moscow, Billy Graham preaching to millions and advising Presidents, Wesley riding 40,000 miles on horseback and preaching in the open air, the gentle theologian Bonhoeffer being hung for plotting to assassinate Hitler. What binds such a diverse group together? Only the generous love of an abundant God. There is no single Christian package.

On the other hand individualism has become a postmodern mantra, a tenet of belief beyond questioning. It is assumed that if we think it is OK, then it is OK. My opinion is as valid as yours; it is only a question of 'what's true for me', we only deal with different 'perspectives' and personal choices. This could mean that my version of Christianity, however bizarre, would be equally as valid as anyone else's. Issues of truth and falsity are finally evacuated. This cannot be the case in a faith which claims that Jesus is the truth (John 14.6), and that the truth (and only the truth) will set us free (John 8.32). Individualism therefore has to be placed in dialogue with the wisdom of the tradition and the teaching of the church. Out of that dynamic will come the beauty of authentic Christian living.

Not rules but a relationship

The core of our Christian living and decision-making, therefore, is not a pre-packed system, but a living relationship with Jesus Christ. The primary question to ask about a proposed course of action, a particular decision or a way of living, is: Does this fit in with my relationship with Christ? How does it look if I put Christ into the picture? Would this be appropriate in the light of my relationship with God and my understanding of him? What we are looking for, in fact, is 'the mind of Christ' (1 Corinthians 2.16).

The principle is the same as in a marriage. If you are married you do not make decisions in isolation from your partner. You view the situation in the light of your relationship, and then decide on what is appropriate. St Augustine went so far as to say 'Love God, and do as you like!' Although that sounds risky, and could be open to abuse, the principle is right. The absolute bond of love at the heart of your life will control your actions. The great thing about this approach is that it is both absolutely safe and wonderfully exhilarating. Our freedom is not the false freedom of anarchy, or the 'Do-It-Yourself' morality which is all that many people are left with today. Our freedom is the genuine opportunity to explore all things that are creative and good, held by the anchor of God's goodness and love.

An Australian schoolboy had come to England for a while and he was in a geography class at school. The teacher was talking about fences and the boy couldn't understand what he meant. 'Fences,' said the teacher, 'You know, lines of wood or wire to keep cattle in the fields.' 'Ah,' said the boy, 'I see what you mean. In Australia we don't have fences; we have wells.' If we are attracted to a place of living water, we do not need to be kept in place by rules and regulations. We are drawn by the goodness on offer at the centre. 'Love God, and do as you like.'

Some tools in the tool bag

We can have confidence, then, that Christian living and decision-making stem from that central relationship with God in Christ. Nevertheless it helps to know that there are some intermediate guidelines around to get us through from that broad central principle to the nitty-gritty of living for God in the world. If we are held and controlled by God's love for us and ours for him, then we will also respect a number of other principles, such as:

✳ the dignity and integrity of people

✳ the centrality of marriage to a secure society

✳ truth-telling

✳ keeping promises

✳ the inviolability of other people's property

✳ the good name of others.

Not that we think in cold logic 'What principles are at stake in this situation?' and then apply the principles as required by our theoretical system. We say much more down-to-earth things to ourselves, such as: 'I should do what I can to help'; 'Marriage is a matter of give and take'; 'Is this letting my friend down?' Nevertheless it is respect for these principles which fleshes out our respect and love for God and his world, even if the way we would put it would be much more prosaic.

We tend to make our decisions out of who we are and what we have become. In a sense it is instinctive. It is even more important therefore that we 'be transformed by the renewing of our minds so that [we] may discern what is the will of God, what is good and acceptable and perfect' (Romans 12.2). We are formed by all sorts of influences, psychological and social, so it is important that as Christians we are formed by the Bible and its values, the traditions of our community, and the wisdom of Christian friends. Then our consciences are being shaped by the Christian story and our decisions come out of a deep history of Christian wisdom. There are some suggestions of books on how to use the Bible and to make decisions in a recognizably Christian way in the Further Reading section at the end of the book. The Bible is the great handbook in all this, but it is not a textbook, or worse, a rule book. We need to soak ourselves in the story and the 'mind' of the Bible, and so to grow in Christian character.

Christians are called to holiness, which is another word for a saint! If that is too scary, think of these words:

The saints were never hurried; they did comparatively few things, and these not necessarily striking or important; and they troubled very little about their influence. Yet they always seemed to hit the mark; every bit of their life told; their simplest actions had a distinction, an exquisiteness which suggest the artist.

(E. Herman, *Creative Prayer*)

Every bit of their life *told*. What a wonderful idea! And it grew naturally out of their relationship with Christ.

Questions for daily life

Living an authentically Christian life presents us with some hard decisions, but if our faith does not work out or help us in the 167 hours every week when we are not in church, then we have to assume it is not much use. Here are some questions to have at the back of our mind, the kind of questions to keep us on track in the rough and tumble of an everyday, working faith.

✳ **Where is God in all this?** We must not allow our Sunday and Monday worlds to become separated. God is there ahead of us in the classroom, the office, the business meeting. Do we actually think of him being there, Lord of the world of work, or do we think we left him at home and in church? So where is God in all this? What is he doing here, and what does he want? If this question is not asked and in some way answered, it is not surprising that many people find their faith to be unreal. But once we can open our minds to the much vaster dimensions of God as he really is, and set him free from his domestication in our home and leisure lives, then the Christian journey becomes much more dangerous and exciting. Let it be a constant question: where is God in all this?

✳ **'What would Jesus do?'** This deceptively simple question has become very common in parts of the United States, and the initials WWJD are to be found on wrist bands, coffee mugs and elsewhere. It may help the teenager caught in a tempting situation, or the person in business who is unclear about the ethics of a particular decision. 'OK, here we are with this issue and it simply is not easy to know what to do for the best. So let's ask a very basic question: what would Jesus do?' Of course we do not know, and it is in a sense presumptuous to pretend we could know. Theologians will tell us, rightly, that there are layers of assumptions in the question. Nevertheless, the very naivety of the question has its own strength. It focuses the mind on finding a recognizably Christian approach to the situation; it puts Christ at the heart of the issue; and it honours the basic principle that we live not by rules but by a relationship with Christ.

✶ **How can I pray about my working life, or life outside church?** Our praying often gets fixed in certain religious categories. We pray for the sick, for activities in the church, for our families, and (usually on Sundays) for countries in the world with special needs. But the rest of life is God's concern just as much as the 'church bits'. How can we pray for all that? Perhaps we could take our diary into our prayer time and pray for colleagues and meetings? Perhaps we could ask for God's help and wisdom with the difficult decisions we have to make at work or elsewhere? And when we are watching the news on television could we at the same time refer those news items on to God? When we are reading the newspaper, we could have half an ear open to the compassion of God, and even as we read, we could be passing on those concerns to the Source of all hope.

✶ **Am I operating with a consistent framework of values?** Or am I making it up as I go along? There is a tendency even amongst committed Christians to work by instinct and hope that by and large we are getting more than half marks. Where do we look for guidance, particularly when people seem to quote the Bible to support all sorts of different positions on, say, living together before marriage, homosexuality, whether warfare can be just, etc.? One place to start in getting a framework is to read over the Ten Commandments as supplemented and interpreted by material from the New Testament. This will not provide all the answers; one cannot sit down and 'read off' the right action from this list. Nevertheless, we can get from this a biblical framework which forms our mind in certain patterns of justice, mercy and love, and this in turn provides an anchor when we try to work out the right response in a particular situation. Here is divine wisdom to return to again and again. It runs as follows:

I am the Lord your God: you shall have no other gods but me.
You shall love the Lord your God with all your heart, with all your soul, with all your mind, and with all your strength.

You shall not make for yourself any idol.

God is spirit, and those who worship him must worship in spirit and truth.

You shall not dishonour the name of the Lord your God.
You shall worship him with awe and reverence.

Remember the Lord's day and keep it holy.
Christ is risen from the dead: set your minds on things that are above, not on things that are on the earth.

Honour your father and mother.
Live as servants of God; honour one another; love the fellowship.

You shall not commit murder.
Be reconciled to your neighbour; overcome evil with good.

You shall not commit adultery.
Know that your body is a temple of the Holy Spirit.

You shall not steal.
Be honest in all that you do and care for those in need.

You shall not be a false witness.
Let everyone speak the truth.

You shall not covet anything which belongs to your neighbour.
Remember the word of the Lord Jesus: It is more blessed to give than to receive. Love your neighbour as yourself, for love is the fulfilling of the law.

* **Where are the tight corners in my life and work, and who would understand?** If we keep God trapped in Sunday-best mode, we run the risk of a disconnected and perhaps even an irrelevant faith. On the other hand, if we can be honest about the difficult areas of our life and open them to the wisdom and mercy of God, there are untold treasures to discover. God is not just a 'good-time God' but a God of infinite resource for our tight corners and problems. Many people work in very stressful situations and feel very near the edge. A young mother may be anxious about her feelings of anger towards her child; a manager in his forties may be feeling he is yesterday's news and be waiting for the redundancy notice; a teacher may be increasingly troubled by constant inspection and pressure from everyone. But where do these people go to discuss these important issues in a context of faith, support and prayer? Sometimes a home group operates in this way, but often the range of people and the other tasks of the group make it less than satisfactory. There is a real need for people under particular pressures to ask themselves who they need to talk to – what individual, fellow teacher, group of teachers, priest etc. would be 'there' for them, helping them to think the issues through *Christianly*, and to pray for them. Those in leadership in local churches should also be on the look out to offer help in setting up that kind of support.

✳ **Am I managing to keep my work, home life and church commitments in balance?** This is a particularly sharp question for many a younger and middle-aged parent who can end up with a sensitive conscience being torn by guilt. So many people become shipwrecked by getting the balance wrong. There are, of course, no pre-packaged answers to the dilemma, but one or two principles are important. First is the need to keep the question under regular review by open family discussions; burying the question and hoping it will resolve itself is no answer. Second, it is valuable to have an honest friend or spiritual companion to give some talking space and some outside feedback. Third, the gospel, and the church which represents it, must never be allowed to induce guilt; the gospel is about liberation, not a new version of law. Fourth, our family is the first church God gives us to belong to and in which to be 'ministers'. God is not glorified by a dysfunctional family.

Help with these questions may come from a variety of sources. Our heritage of scripture, reason and the experience of the church is a rich resource, but a biblical-formed mind does not emerge overnight. In the meantime, two particularly helpful sources of Christian reflection on living out our faith in work situations are:

✳ The Ridley Hall Foundation, Ridley Hall, Cambridge CB3 9HG.

✳ God@Work, London Bible College, Green Lane, Northwood, Middlesex HA6 2UW.

A very useful workbook is from Richard Higginson, *Mind the Gap* (Church Pastoral Aid Society, 1997).

Money, sex and power

Those three words represent a minefield of issues for any responsible person, and in particular, anyone waiting to follow Christ with integrity. Let no Christian ever suppose he or she has sorted them all out! We are all caught in the slipstream of powerful forces in our culture and in ourselves, and we need grace and humility to handle these difficult issues well.

Our culture is fascinated and obsessed with the 'big three' – money, sex and power. To read the Sunday newspapers, both tabloid and broadsheet, you wouldn't think there was much else of significance to consider except sport and a little personality politics. Christians swim in the same cultural sea as everyone else and feel the same pressures. Moreover, they are made of the same emotions and drives as others, and have experienced the same damage. Sydney Smith's jibe about the three sexes, 'men, women, and clergymen', will not do! As one poet said, all of us 'wobble 'twixt muck and a golden crown'.

What Christians might hope for is not exemption from the exam but some guiding principles and a clear head. And of course that controlling relationship with Christ. Even to attempt to offer any guidance in these hugely complex areas in just a few lines is like answering the problem of evil on the back of an envelope. Yet not to write something in this crucial area would be unacceptably cowardly! All that is offered here are some basic Christian guidelines which, in common with the rest of this book, only scratch the surface, but hopefully scratch in the right area.

Money

✳ **'All things come from you'** we say in the Communion service. Everything is a gift, ultimately coming from the hands of God. Although we earn our salaries by good, honest toil, the deepest truth about that money is that is is part of the gift of life itself, without which nothing is earned anyway. Like everything else, it is on loan from God for us to use well.

✳ **'The love of money is a root of all kinds of evil.'** (1 Timothy 6.10) Note 'the *love* of', not money in itself. Money is morally neutral; it serves as a means of exchanging goods and services in society. The problem comes when we hold on to money with closed fists; we are then incapable of receiving anything else. The danger is that acquiring wealth is like drinking sea water; the more we have the thirstier we get.

✳ **'You will always be rich enough to be generous.'** (2 Corinthians 9.11) Or, 'Money is like muck; no good unless it be spread around.' The wealth which we have on loan from God is to be used for others as well as ourselves. Paul writes in 2 Corinthians chapters 8 and 9 about our responsibility to share what we have received. He is absolutely straight with the Corinthians, but also realistic: 'Each person should give as he has decided for himself; there should be no reluctance, no sense of compulsion; God loves a cheerful giver.' (2 Corinthians 9.7) The rub comes with deciding how much should be given. Try these principles:

1 It is essential to give first and not last. We have to give what is right and not what is 'left', for the simple reason that there is never enough left at the end of the day. Give first, and the rest of our expenditure fits in.

2 'Our gift is acceptable according to what we have, not according to what we do not have.' (2 Corinthians 8.12) In other words – be realistic. But remember how impressed Jesus was by the widow who crept into the Temple and in her 'mite' gave far more proportionately than the apparent big givers (Luke 21.1–4).

3 Christians have often talked about the biblical tithe of 10 per cent of income. Because the biblical world did not have taxes and National Insurance which now, in a sense, do some of our charitable work for us, others talk about 5 per cent of income. We need to remember, however, that the New Testament standard does not seem to be based on any figure; the standard is 'sheer generousity': 'For you know the grace of our Lord Jesus Christ, that though he was rich, yet for our sakes he became poor so that you, through his poverty, might become rich.' (2 Corinthians 8.9)

4 A wise old clergyman used to say: 'Think of the figure you want to give – and then double it!' Afterwards you knew he was right!

* **Adopt a simpler lifestyle.** There can be no rules about this, but the vital element is that of pitching our lifestyle thoughtfully rather than seeing acquisitiveness and disposability as good, because they are convenient. We all need to examine the way we use scarce resources. Do we always need to take the car? Do we leave the lights on? Do we get rid of things because we want the latest model? Do we buy environmentally friendly goods as far as possible? How seriously do we recycle? Do we take our unneeded clothes to charity shops? In a world as fragile as ours these questions become serious for everyone, but especially for Christians who understand that men and women have been given responsibility as stewards of creation (see Genesis 1). On the other hand this should not make us grim, life-denying fanatics. Our religion should bring us to life, and where it fails to do this we can be sure that we are somehow missing the point.

✳ **Our wealth, such as it is, should be neither a defence nor a weapon, but a grace.** It can be a defence when we buy things as a way of coping with life's problems – so-called 'retail therapy'. It can be a weapon when we use our wealth to keep out those who are poorer than ourselves and mix only with our own social and economic equals. The Corinthian church got into this divisiveness over the meal they had before the Lord's Supper. The rich went ahead with their Fortnum and Mason hampers and the poor looked on (1 Corinthians 11.18–22). Our wealth should be neither a defence nor a weapon but a grace, to receive and to give. We are called to receive everything from God's hands and then live responsibly and generously with others. In this way, money is a kind of touchstone of faith. Commitment is not only spelt r-i-s-k, it is also spelt m-o-n-e-y.

✳ **Keep money in its place!** Financial matters have a habit of controlling agendas, even church agendas. Churches have to keep money in its place as the servant of spiritual goals. It may be a little too easy to say that 'what God orders, he also pays for', but it remains true that if we get the gospel priorities right then the finance usually follows. However, manipulation of all sorts is out of order. The members of a church met to discuss the question of repairs to the roof. A wealthy member stood up and said he would give £500. As he sat down a piece of ceiling fell on his head. He rose again and said he would make it £5,000. Another member was then heard to say, 'Hit him again, Lord!'

Sex

What we will focus on here is really quite specific. It is the place of sexual activity in the God-given scheme of things. I will not tackle the sociology of sex, sex and gender, sexual abuse, sexual politics, sex and the cinema, sex and the page-three girl, or a hundred other ways that society links sex to everything it can spell! Straightforward sexual activity is complex enough. Here are some principles.

✳ **Sex is sensational and therefore too good to mess up.** We need to remember that God invented sex along with the rest of the created world: 'God saw all that he had made and it was very good.' (Genesis 1.31) The darker side of Christian tradition which has been suspicious of sex has in fact been paying a back-handed compliment to the power and the glory of sex. It is so good, so overwhelming and so satisfying that it came to be seen as a threat to our worship of God alone. The better approach is not to put God and sex in opposition to each other but to place sex correctly within the genius and care of God. Placed there, sex is truly to be celebrated as a glorious gift.

❋ **Sex is a relational gift and not a functional one.** In other words it is about the celebrating and confirming of relationship rather than the functional pursuit of orgasm. The linkage between sex and relationship is the central core of a Christian understanding of sex, and at the same time the dimension under greatest threat in our society. Sex is increasingly seen as a pleasurable experience which two people can share without commitment or consequence, and the results of this social experiment are only just beginning to emerge. Paul writes of our body being 'a temple of the Holy Spirit, who is in you' (1 Corinthians 6.19). If people see their bodies less as a temple and more as an amusement arcade, the final cost in terms of self-worth and ability to sustain faithful long-term relationships may turn out to be huge. Perhaps the young will learn from their elders' mistakes. A friend of mine was sitting with a group of young people when, apropros of nothing at all, the 10-year-old sitting next to him said: 'You know John, there's far too much recreational sex going on these days.' Out of the mouths of babes . . .

❋ **The Bible sees full sex as appropriate in certain relationships and not in others.** The crucial mark of difference is a covenant. Just as God called for a full and faithful relationship with his covenant people, so he looked for full and faithful relationships amongst his followers. If 'covenant relationship' is the key model for Christians then certain guidelines follow. Relationships are not all-or-nothing experiences. They grow and develop, and as they do so the sexual dimension of the relationship should grow and develop too. The physical side of the relationship should match the emotional and spiritual. The guideline is *appropriateness*. This would mean that full sexual relations are appropriate when the full commitment to permanence and faithfulness is made. Individual Christian couples have to work out what this means for them. They may use guidelines such as, 'Only do what you can discuss', or, 'Is this actually selfish?' or, 'Would I mind having a baby with this person?' But the key factor is that sex is relational and not functional; it relates to the stage of the couple's interdependence, not to the level of their personal need for sex.

❊ **Sex is ultimately sacramental.** It creates and sustains the deepest personal union between couples, and gives them a means of representing the beauty and significance of their relationship. Sex is an outward and visible sign to each other of the desire to share everything, and to live with and for the other person. It expresses delight, respect and hope. It offers a lifelong way of celebrating love and commitment, and it enables couples to explore intimacy, play, foolishness and forgiveness. No wonder it's sensational! But it also has the fragility of all precious things. Sex is therefore most safe and most splendid when we follow the Maker's instructions.

❊ **Sex is creative,** not only of relationship, as described above, but also, most fundamentally, it is creative of new life – a baby. It therefore calls for the highest degree of responsibility on the part of those making love. Bringing a new life into the world is a task to be undertaken with awe – not perhaps in the moment of love-making when passion and abandon is rather more likely than awe! – but certainly in the intention of the act itself. Sex is creative by its very internal dynamic. Indeed, sex should always be about discovery – discovery of life, of joy, of sacred 'bodiliness', or of the miracle of making a brand new life.

❊ **Christians may be particularly vulnerable** in the area of sex unless they are prepared to be very honest and humble. Many churches have been badly damaged when an affair is discovered in the heart of the church's life. It often seems that Christians feel they are above the problems the rest of society gets into over sex. We are not supposed to have those problems; we have put them in the hands of God. However, if we put down a cardboard floor to keep out the lions who live in the basement we should not be surprised if one day they get out and rampage around the house. A Desert Father of the early church once reported to his spiritual guide that he had finally overcome all sexual passion inside himself. The guide looked at him and said firmly: 'Then go back and pray to be tempted again!' Passion is natural; it is part of our humanity to struggle with our sexuality, and in the struggle to become a more mature and integrated individual. Pretending the lions are safe in the basement is no answer.

✳ **Read the Song of Songs in the Old Testament** and be reminded that God is both earthy and heavenly in this business of sex! Can we share both his idealism and his realism?

Power

Perhaps we think that whereas money and sex are immediately relevant to us, power is one thing we do not need to worry about because we do not have any! Unfortunately we cannot avoid the issue so easily. We exercise power in our family whether as a child or a parent. We exercise power at work whether as an employer or an employee. We exercise power over our friends whether benignly or manipulatively. We exercise power with our spending, with our vote, with our membership of church committees. Think about it!

It is fairly clear to see in the New Testament that Jesus was much harder on those who abused their power (particularly religious power) than he was on those who got into a mess with their sexuality. Compare his terrifying treatment of the teachers and pharisees in Matthew 23 with his gentle treatment of the woman caught in the act of adultery in John 8. Power as a whole is a hugely ambiguous subject. It can be constructive; it can be dangerous. It can be overt; it can be hidden. It can be over-used or under-used. So, what guidelines are to be found in the Bible and in Christian tradition?

✳ **Power belongs to God and we are his agents.** The Bible recognizes only one source of power and authority. Whether as a parent or a politician, we need to be sure we remember that we only have authority on behalf of Another. Kings and princes only rule by divine permission, and indeed even 'enemy' kings are used by God for his purposes (Cyrus of Persia is one such: Isaiah 45.1). In that lovely incident when Jesus is asked to give a judgement on whether tax should be paid to the Emperor, he subverts the trickery of the question by reminding them that everything, but everything, belongs to God. He is not some distant rival to Caesar, a long-forgotten great uncle who turns up at the last moment to claim his share of the cake. If God is God at all then he is God of everything, and no one has any authority except by divine permission. 'Give to Caesar what belongs to Caesar (that's fair enough; he has a job to do), but give to God what belongs to God' – which is nothing short of everything. So power belongs to God – and we are his agents.

✻ **Power is pervasive and needs to be understood.** Christians should not be naive in this area, believing that nasty things like power-plays, manipulation, abuse of power, subversion, unholy alliances and so on, do not occur in churches. We are simply too polite to call them that. Just go to a church council meeting, sit back and observe what is really going on! The reality is that power is always being exercised, benevolently or not, in families and offices as well as in governments, police forces and legal systems, and we do well to ask the question often: Where is the power operating in this situation? Who is doing what here, to whom, and why? This is not to pre-judge the way that power is being used; it is simply to understand some of the dynamics. Who has the power in this church meeting? Is it the vicar, who is making all the noise? Or the vicar's wife (or husband), the unseen presence? Or the treasurer, who keeps shaking his head over his figures? Or 'the awkward squad' at the back of the meeting?

When Pilate had Jesus standing before him and said that he had the power to free Jesus or to kill him, Jesus pointed out, quite rightly, that Pilate was talking through his hat. 'You would have no power over me if it were not given you from above.' (John 19.10–12) We have to recognize where the power really lies before we can work with it or against it.

✻ **Power is morally neutral but potentially corrupting.** Power has an equal potential for good and evil, and everything in between. The problem is that experience shows that power tends to corrupt those who hold it, mainly because power provides a neat hook for 'original sin' to hang its coat on. Original sin means that there is no part of ourselves or our structures which is immune from going wrong. And power offers a perfect vehicle for that process. One of the tasks of the church in society, therefore, is to exercise a healthy critique of those with power. Martin Luther King talked of the church being 'creatively maladjusted' to many of the structures of society. The other side of that coin is to be in 'critical solidarity' with those in power, but either way, the task is clear – to be the moral conscience of those who, by divine permission, exercise power at a particular time and place. And Christians are called to do that at all levels – workplace, local government, school governors, church, even their own family.

❊ **Power can be exercised wonderfully to transform society.** And that is the chief purpose of it. God gives us his permission to exercise that power so that through us he can make 'the kingdom of the world to be the kingdom of our Lord and of his Christ' (Revelation 11.15). Each of us is in a position of power, and some of us will be in positions of really quite considerable influence in society, either now or later in life. The question we need to have before us is the question of goals: Where are we trying to go in this organization/church/school? Are our aims high and straight? Are our methods true and transparent? Above all, does this look and feel like God's way? Many pressure groups in our society can be excellent vehicles for Christians wanting to work for the transformation of society. Christian Aid, Greenpeace, Amnesty and a host of others give us the opportunity to put our ideals into practical action.

❊ **Power should be used non-violently.** We follow a leader who declared that 'those who live by the sword will die by the sword' (Matthew 26.52). However, the record of the church in emulating the young Prince of Peace has not been good. Moreover, who has not seen the first reports of strikes in the Falklands War, the Gulf War, the Serbian/Kosovo campaign and other recent conflicts and not felt a sinking feeling that this still seems to be the best we can do to sort out international disagreements? The Christian way is essentially non-violent. Whether it gets to a bottom line where violence is the only strategy left, will be up to the moral conscience of different Christians. But it has to be somewhat alarming that Christian attitudes to war and violence seem to be little dissimilar to those of the rest of the population. Gandhi, that great prophet of non-violence, was once asked what he thought of Western civilization. 'I think it would be a very good idea,' he said. And yet that civilization has been built on the heritage of the Prince of Peace, who knew that a deeper answer to the world's woes was to absorb the violence that assaulted him and bury it in the depths of his Father's heart. Even if we would ultimately pick up the sword to protect our loved ones from evil, Christians should be known for their longer fuse, their alternative strategies, and their radical trust in God.

Thinking Christianly – a method

Imagine that you are faced with an issue which is causing you or your family or church a degree of perplexity. This is not just ordinary day-to-day decision-making. This is when you are trying to think out whether to go for a major redevelopment of the church for worship and community use, but the costs are vast and the energy needed is equally daunting. Or it might be that you are perplexed about the threat of Western military action in the Middle East, or about proposed changes in the law on euthanasia or genetic cloning. You may be facing a dilemma at work where confidentiality and underhand dealings are pointing in different directions with you caught in the middle. The question is: How do you think Christianly about these situations? How can you approach the complexities of the issue without either appearing blinkered and dogmatic, on the one hand, or just to be going with the popular secular flow, on the other?

One answer is to use a straightforward method of Christian or theological thinking which is at the heart of the enterprise of what we call 'practical theology'. The method is often referred to as 'the pastoral cycle', and it offers an approach which honours both the uniqueness of the particular problem and the wisdom of the Christian heritage. The pastoral cycle is a structured way of thinking about complex issues. It is a way of learning from experience, and then planning a considered response. As a basic approach it is used in many disciplines apart from practical theology, such as education, training and management, but while the process might be held in common, the content will obviously vary according to the discipline.

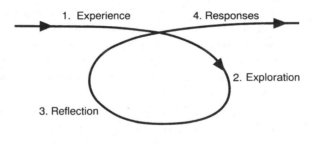

Figure 3

The method

The pastoral cycle has four main phases (Figure 3):

1 **Experiencing the situation.** Your brother has just left his wife and young child to go and live with another woman. You are immensely cross with him but do not know whether a tough stance or a

conciliatory, 'counselling' stance is the best approach. Or you have a job opportunity in another part of the country but the cost would involve taking your partner and child out of the environment in which they are very happy, or leaving them behind while you commute at weekends. In both cases the particularities of the situation need to be understood as clearly as possible. All the facts need to be out in the open so that it is not possible later to say, 'Well, if I'd only known that, it might have been different.' We need to get the story right.

2 **Exploring or analysing.** At this stage you need to analyse the situation with as much objectivity as possible. This involves seeking to understand the motivations of your brother, the dynamics of his marriage, the implications of his leaving, financially, emotionally and socially. In the other situation, what are your own motives? What are the longer-term implications of taking the new job or staying where you are? What are the company's strategies and motives? And so on. This exploration stage should not be skimped because it seeks to bring out as much clarity and objectivity as possible and to hold up the rush into a response which is driven by emotion and the desire to 'get the problem sorted out'. Talking to other people, writing it all down, gathering information from other sources, are all part of this stage of exploration.

3 **Christian reflection.** This is the stage when we bring in the resources of faith, the Bible, theology, the wisdom of the church. Of course we will be praying about the whole process all along, but if we bring in the other Christian resources too early we run the risk of foreclosing the argument without having properly understood the nature of the situation or the other factors involved. Christians have often assumed they have understood complex situations and applied 'formula answers' from the Bible or even perhaps plain prejudice, and this has done no service to the truth nor to the credibility of the church in the eyes of others.

At this stage, however, thoughtful Christian reflection will ask questions like these:

✱ Where is God in all this? Where is his voice to be heard? Where will he be feeling the pain? What kind of questions would he be asking, and of whom?

✱ Is there some part of the Christian story, particularly in the Bible, which illuminates this situation? Perhaps in the first situation described above, it might be the woman taken in adultery, the story of Hosea and his wife, or Peter's betrayal of Jesus. Or are there some great themes from Christian thinking which seem to resonate with what is going on here? Perhaps it might be the themes of covenant, faithfulness, sin, hope, crucifixion and resurrection.

* Where is the power being exercised here? Is it being exercised fairly, and what would be a Christian response? In considering that job in another part of the country are you using or abusing your legitimate responsibility in the family? How does your partner get a proper lever on the situation? What does this discussion say about the way authority works out in your family?

* What is the Christ-like thing to do here? Beneath and behind all the rational arguments, what feels to be most in accord with the spirit of Christ?

4 **Responding.** Out of the process of gathering the facts and the emotions of the situation, exploring them accurately, and reflecting on them Christianly, we should come to a greater confidence in responding appropriately as Christians. There will not be a 'right answer' which God was keeping from us until we can break the code. His guidance does not work on such a mischievous basis! Through prayer and responsible thinking, God gives us the wisdom to make decisions, and he then gives us the grace and persistence to see them through. By using the deliberate process of the pastoral cycle we may be kept from 'knee-jerk' reactions and be able to make more authentically Christian responses. The whole cycle should not become a chore, however, or a wooden exercise in self-justification. Hopefully it might become a swift and instinctive way of handling certain situations. The point, however, is that there is here a structured approach to complex life-situations which in one form or another ought to be considered with honesty and faith.

Knowing God's guidance

Here is a complex area, and one which gets Christians tied up in knots! How does God guide us? How can we know we are doing his will? It seems rather important that we do that will, but our experience is that God does not write things in the sky for us, or thunder unmistakably in our ear or even send us a spare heavenly host to make it quite clear. But why should it be so difficult if we have a God who loves us and longs for our well-being?

One important first point is to be clear that God is not trying to be difficult! He does not set us spiritual brain-teasers for which we need to crack the code in order to get the answer God knows all along. Nor does he want us to try ridiculous tricks to get the guidance we want, like the young Christian who said he had gone to South America because when he was looking for guidance he had suddenly seen a bar of chocolate with Brazil nuts in it. His sceptical friend asked him, 'What would you have done if it had been a Mars bar?'

A second point to note is that the Bible never talks about guidance; it only talks about a Guide. This Guide is also the Comforter, the Holy Spirit, the one who will lead us into the truth (John 16.13). Guidance is not absract; it is personal. If you are lost in a strange city and you stop your car to ask the way, you might receive the answer, 'No problem. Turn first right, fourth left, through six sets of traffic lights, right at the second roundabout, bear left at the Dog and Vomit, then look for a man in a bright orange anorak – ask him.' Your heart sinks as you drive off. But then you might ask another person. 'Certainly,' he says, 'I'm going there myself. Let me hop in beside you.' Now you drive off with complete confidence because you have, not guidance, but a Guide.

If we say that God has a plan for our lives it suggests that if we get it wrong at any point and make the wrong decision, then our lives will go haywire. It would be like a crossword puzzle where there is only one right answer and a mistake would nullify all the rest of the puzzle. A better understanding would be to say that God does not have a plan but rather a vision for our lives. He sees the person we can become and sets about helping us to get there. This means that there are many routes to the vision – some undoubtedly better than others – but God will use every decision we make and keep us moving towards the goal of maturity in Christ ('the measure of the stature of the fulness of Christ': Ephesians 4.13). This is a much more dynamic and relational view of guidance than a wooden 'right or wrong answer' approach.

Guidance, therefore, is seeking the best route for God's vision for our lives to be achieved. It will not be the only route, but we will always be looking for the most effective next step of the journey.

Some guidelines

∗ **Think, watch and pray.** God's guidance often comes to us in the form of 'loud thoughts' which come through our minds as we think hard, attentively and prayerfully. It is not sufficient just to pray and then to leave it all to God. That would be like putting in our contact lenses and then closing our eyes, confident that the lenses would do the trick! The lenses actually help the task of seeing well, and praying helps the task of thinking well. There is such a thing as 'sanctified common sense' and perhaps Christians should use more of it!

* **Take the Bible seriously.** Scripture gives us very important general principles for our decision-making. We cannot say certain things about theft, greed, revenge, adultery and so on, as if God is equivocal about them. He has been uncomfortably clear! We need to develop a 'biblically formed mind,' which responds instinctively to the parameters set by the Bible. Moreover, when it comes to specific guidance it is remarkable how often our regular reading of the Bible will seem extraordinarily appropriate to the circumstances of our own life and decisions. God uses his Word to speak to our hearts and minds if we are used to listening out for him by regular, prayerful Bible reading.

* **Trust the Holy Spirit.** Jesus says that his followers will recognize his voice (John 10.4–5), and so the Holy Spirit is often the voice of Christ in our lives, guiding us along. We may feel a strong compulsion or direction as we pray. We may have a growing conviction about a course of action, a growing warmth about it – or indeed the opposite. Our prayer, of course, should draw us towards God's best way, not draw him towards ours. When a ship comes into dock the ropes are thrown to the quay so that the ship is pulled into shore, not so that the shore is pulled towards the ship! As we pray, our minds should become clearer as we are drawn towards the mind of Christ.

* **Talk to other trusted friends.** God works through other people and the Bible has a principle that where two or three witnesses agree then a course of action is to be followed (Matthew 18.16). 'Make plans by seeking advice.' (Proverbs 20.18). Of course the advisers must be chosen carefully. They must be people of wisdom and not chosen mainly because they are likely to agree with our own desired course of action! Friends will naturally have their own prejudices and unexamined assumptions as well – we need to listen out for which advice has about it the ring of God's truth.

* **Try the doors.** Sometimes we need to push at a door to see if it opens. In a profound sense 'God is in the facts', and we can trust that certain things will come together for us and certain doors will open, and others, rightly, will not. It is also the experience of many people

that next to a closed door will be an open door because God never leaves us in an airtight room. The open door, of course, may well lead us to continue on our present course. Be patient and the right course will usually emerge, although we have to remember that we must play our part and be actively committed to seeking God's best way in order for him to guide us. You can't change the course of an ocean liner if it is at anchor; it has to be moving in order to be redirected.

Guidance therefore is not a magical mystery tour around the convolutions of God's mischievous will. It is opening our minds and hearts to the wisdom of God, and letting other people, and the facts themselves, help us in that discernment.

They said that

In Jesus' society there is a new way to live:
    you show wisdom by trusting people,
    you handle leadership by serving,
    you handle offenders by forgiving,
    you handle money by sharing,
    you handle enemies by loving,
    and you handle violence by suffering.   SOURCE UNTRACED

When Christ calls a man, he bids him come and die.
DIETRICH BONHOEFFER

When we fail in our discipleship it is always for one of two reasons: either we are not trying to be loyal, or else we are trying in our own strength.   WILLIAM TEMPLE

The disciples were carried along by the vitality of a leader whose presence brought God so near, and made his will so clear, that it was like living in heaven already.   JOHN V. TAYLOR

According to the theory of aerodynamics, and as may be readily demonstrated by means of a wind tunnel, the bumble bee is unable to fly. This is because the size, weight and shape of his body in relation to the total wing span makes flight impossible. But the bumble bee, being

ignorant of these scientific facts and possessing considerable
determination, does fly – and makes a little honey too.
FRANCIS CLIFFORD

I believe in Christianity as I believe the sun has risen, not only because I
see it, but because by it, I see everything else.   C. S. LEWIS

For good you are and bad, and like to coins
Some true, some light, but every one of you
Stamped with the image of the King.   TENNYSON

There is never a pause, O Christ, in your persistent question, 'who do
you say that I am?' You are he who loves me into life unending; each
morning anew you slip onto my finger the ring of the prodigal son
recovered, the ring of festival. Always you urged – live that little part of
the gospel that you have already grasped. Proclaim my life among men.
Kindle fire on the earth. You, follow me . . .   BROTHER ROGER OF TAIZÉ

6 Moving on

What to do when things go wrong

Every Christian has times when their spiritual journey seems to sink into the sand. It may be that God seems terribly remote and prayers seem to bounce back off the ceiling. It may be that going to church has become a chore and a secular Sunday with the newspaper and a pub lunch seems much more attractive. It may be that a kind of deadness seems to lie at the heart of our spiritual life, and the promise of Christ to bring us 'life in all its fullness' seems a mockery or a distant memory. The Christian life seems unreal and demanding, and if we're honest, Christian people are beginning to get up our nose! Has the whole enterprise been in vain? Was it all emotion, whistling happy tunes in the dark? Shall we give it all up?

* **Don't panic!** Everyone goes through something like this at some stage. There are things that can be done. And if you want just one verse to hang on to, try this: 'God is faithful: he will not let you be tempted beyond what you can bear. But when you are tempted, he will also provide a way out.' (1 Corinthians 10.13)

* **Don't feel guilty.** Guilt is one of the first responses Christians often have. It is the sign of a sensitive conscience, and better than the secular world's refusal to accept responsibility for anything, but nevertheless it can be badly overdone in Christian circles. Guilt usually paralyses the will. What we need instead is a cool look at what is really going on, and why God seems to have gone absent without leave.

* **Beware of your feelings.** Feelings are at best an unreliable guide to our well-being. A drunk up a lamp-post may feel very good about the

world, but a better guide to reality would be the policeman on the pavement! Bad feelings too can be the result of anything from poor health to a poor digestion. Problems at work, difficulties with children, an impending move, stress, financial worries – all these can affect our emotional balance. A simple illustration of a train may help those who can remember what a guard's van is! The train consists of an engine called **Facts**, which pulls a carriage called **Faith**, which may or may not be pulling a guard's van called **Feelings**. The Facts of Christianity can travel by themselves; we travel in the carriage called Faith; but the guard's van of Feelings is an optional extra!

✳ **Try to analyse where the malaise is coming from.** When we feel low, we often experience problems as a great lump. We are overwhelmed by the intractability, the 'lumpishness' of them. The first step is to try to divide the lump up into its constituent elements. It helps to recognize what might be the multifaceted nature of the problem and to divide responsibility appropriately. Are we feeling low because of a number of other factors as exampled above? Are we simply tired out? Are we feeling angry with someone (our partner? the vicar? God?), and are we also just being a bit lazy spiritually? In other words, try and spread the problem out into its constituent parts. Then you can take action on each of them.

Sometimes the malaise comes from a depressive condition, and Christians often suffer from a double-bind at this point. Not only are they depressed but they feel that, as Christians, they should not be that way! Depression, however, is an all too common and wholly natural affliction with multiple causes. Christians are no more exempt from depression than from the common cold. Jesus did not promise his followers success, good health and a bulging bank account – he promised them joy and a cross. Depression needs to be treated by the usual combination of medical and spiritual help. Those who suffer need to be assured that God loves them as much as ever (that is, totally), and that they should hang on in there because God is committed to a strategy of resurrection.

✳ **Go back to where you lost the plot.** Most of us have some well-tried path of prayer or Bible reading where we know we have been refreshed and fed in the past. Perhaps we should go back to a structured form of prayer and Bible-reading notes, where the framework is clear and some at least of the work is already done for us. It may be as well that we are lacking *input*. We may be going round in our own circles and to read short extracts from a spiritual writer will give us some energy to get moving again. Of course, going back to safe ground may not always be the right thing. We may have been moved on by God to new spiritual pastures and the old ground would be as lifeless as the desert we are in at present. In this case, the next suggestion may apply.

* **Move on to new territory.** If the old ways have gone dead then God may be calling us on to some new exploration of the Spirit. This book has lots of different approaches to the central Christian actions of prayer and Bible reading; we might try one which is new to us. We have used Bible-reading notes, but have we tried Ignatian meditation? We have long prayed freestyle but have we tried a simple Daily Office? Or we might try taking on a new challenge at church, or a new way of working out our daily discipleship, as in the other sections of the book. It may be that God is saying to us that the grass has been fully cropped in the old pastures. 'Come on up to new pastures, to the higher mountains. Take a risk!'

* **Talk to someone about the problem.** That person may be a good confidential friend, or your own vicar or minister, or simply a person you know instinctively will understand. Have the courage to go and ask for a chat; they will be privileged that you are prepared to seek their help. The person you are looking for is not someone who will jump in with their advice after five minutes! You want someone who will listen patiently and help you clarify the issues, and at the appropriate time might suggest a range of possible ways forward for you to choose from. There is also a wonderful tradition in the church of spiritual companions or 'spiritual directors'. There is more about them in the next section.

* **Be patient.** We live in an age of 'quick fixes'. If something goes wrong with the washing machine, the car, or the computer we expect to be able to call someone in to sort it out straightaway. This expectation has stretched into health care where we expect physicians and surgeons to 'fix' a malfunctioning body. The danger is that this attitude is also creeping into relationships and thence into spirituality. It simply is not the case that damaged relationships can be mended like a computer which has crashed. Nor can we fix our relationship with God by a few new techniques. Relationships grow; they are organic; they breathe; they develop and take new turns; they build

slowly and sometimes take false directions. So our relationship with God must be treated with patience, as well as confidence. Patience, because it is a relationship; confidence, because it is God, the loving Father who longs for his prodigals to return. There is no doubt at all of God's love and mercy, and of his complete faithfulness as we seek to get into the dance with him again. He will always be close, even as we learn the steps, and even if we are not aware of his loving presence.

✻ **Be aware of the 'cloud of unknowing' and the 'dark night of the soul'.** It is just possible that something deeper still is going on in our experience of being in a spiritual desert. The concepts of the cloud of unknowing and the dark night of the soul should not be introduced too soon or too cheaply. It is much more likely that some of the explanations above are responsible for our malaise. It is worth remembering, however, that some people are drawn on to a state of darkness where the cloud of unknowing between us and God can only be pierced by the 'dart of longing love', or where the night of the senses and the dark night of the soul are the characteristic experience of those few people whose ascent to God has involved the stripping away of all supports, on the way to an utter transparency to God and his grace. This mystical path is nothing like the experience of a Christian whose prayer life has gone soggy, but he should note this last possibility for the sake of completeness. Good translations of *The Cloud of Unknowing* and the works of St John of the Cross are available from Christian bookshops, but it would be good to talk to a wise spiritual guide before embarking on this line of thought and prayer.

✻ **Don't give up – ever!** The promise is too great. The stakes are high.

Moving on in prayer

This book is about getting going, or beginning again, in the basic arts of Christian living. Prayer, therefore, is central. The journey we embark on, however, is a lifetime of living prayer and so a word or two might help as we look to moving on further.

A spiritual companion

Whether such a person is called a spiritual director, a soul friend or simply a companion on the way, does not matter. What does matter is the principle of having someone to whom we are spiritually accountable and who will give us the unconditional freedom to say whatever we like about our journey of faith and life. Such a person will help us to clarify our thinking, interpret what is going on, and suggest new lines of thought or new ways to follow. They will both accept us and confront us. They will give us space to be fearful and time to spin dreams. They will be on our side and help us to discern what God is doing with us. What a gift!

Finding such a person is more difficult. Your church at local or regional level may have someone who acts as a 'clearing house' for such needs. Your own priest or minister may be able to suggest someone. (It is usually best to go beyond your local church to find the right person.) You may instinctively know that someone you have come across is the person to ask. Always have an exploratory meeting or two to see if the relationship is going to 'gel', and review it every year. Meeting three or four times a year might be enough for one person, and monthly might not be enough for another. Feel your way to what is right and then trust that relationship as a very special gift from God.

Going on retreat

More and more people are coming to see the profound value of going away to a quiet place to give proper time and space to their inner world and their spiritual journey. It gives God time to sort out our jangled lives, to reprioritize, to have a spiritual bath. There is no pressure to do or be anything. No one sets an exam. But the benefits are enormous and will spill over into everything else we do.

These are some of the things to note:

* **Finding the right place.** There may be somewhere local that some of your friends know of and go to themselves. Alternatively the National Retreat Association produce an annual 80-page magazine listing all the places and retreats around the country, with all necessary details for enquiry and booking. It is called *Retreats* and is available from many Christian bookshops or direct from Central Hall, 256 Bermondsey Street, London SE1 3UJ (tel. 0171 357 7736).

* **Choosing the retreat.** You could go on one that is led by an experienced retreat conductor, or to a place where you could see a member of the community occasionally during your stay. Or you could just go and use the time and space by yourself. Silence is usually a major component of a retreat so you would need to be clear

about the parameters of that silence – how much is expected or possible.

✳ **Leave behind** all unfinished work, all those reports and articles you promised yourself you would read, and all the highly organized timetables and lists of what you want to do. There need be no sense of 'ought' about a retreat. You might also leave behind any expectations of a 'big experience'. The heavenly host rarely turn up on demand, and in any case it is in the small voice, the gentle touch, the little reminder, that God will very often give you the most.

✳ **What to do.** Join in the prayers of the community. Drop into the timeless rhythm of their services. Make time for your own prayers in order to lay out your life before God. Take a book or two that you have wanted to read, or has been recommended to you. Take a notebook to write down your feelings and experiences, or to jot down a special thought or a wild idea. Take some exercise, and get plenty of sleep.

✳ **Spiritually** be open to whatever God gives. Try to use your senses and be aware of what you are usually too busy to notice. Move more slowly and with greater awareness of what is going on around you and within you. Give yourself over to the whole experience. Be honest with yourself and with God. And remember – don't push the river; it flows by itself!

Groups and celebrations

It is often noted that for Christians to grow spiritually is seems best to be active at four levels, each of which feeds us in a different way:

✳ the individual – for our bedrock relationship with God;

✳ the small group – for fellowship, discussion, questioning, support, prayer;

✳ the congregation – for public worship with the church family;

✳ the celebration – for inspiration and a shot in the arm.

The individual and the congregational levels speak for themselves. The small group could be one of many varieties, from a home group to a silent prayer group (often called Julian groups after Mother Julian of Norwich, a fourteenth-century mystic). The celebration could again be of many forms, such as a big Songs of Praise service in a cathedral or a week at the Taizé community in France, or the giant Spring Harvest, Soul Survivor or New Wine events which have become so popular in recent years. For more information, contact:

✻ Taizé, 71250 Taizé Community, France.

✻ Spring Harvest, 14 Horsted Square, Uckfield TN22 1QL.

✻ Soul Survivor, 7 Greycaine Rd., Watford WD2 4JP.

✻ New Wine, 37 Quickley Lane, Chorleywood, Rickmansworth WD3 5AE.

Prayer and personality

There has been considerable interest recently in the way that different personalities are drawn to different types of prayer (see chapter 2). Knowledge of these links does not function as a limitation on people but serves to explain some of the reasons why they feel drawn to particular forms of spirituality, and with that knowledge of 'home' can come a greater confidence to go on journeys of the spirit. The two workshops which offer particular help in this area are based on:

✻ the Myers-Briggs Personality Type Indicator, using Jungian insights

✻ the Enneagram, an ancient system of self-discovery.

Details of workshops can be found in the publication *Retreats*, as above.

Spiritual axes

Figure 4 is intended to help you get some overview of your spiritual preferences in the areas of prayer and worship. It offers a visual method of assessing the 'shape' of your spirituality at this moment, and the opportunity to reflect on the implications.

Exercise

At either end of each axis are words which represent approximate opposites. For example, 'individual' is opposite 'corporate' so that you can think where you would place yourself along that axis in terms of preferring individual or corporate worship. Do other people clutter up your worship or are they essential to it? Is it a small Communion or a large Morning Service at which you feel most at home? Put a mark at that point on the line which represents your position on those questions. And similarly on all the other axes.

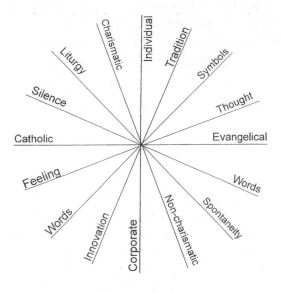

Figure 4 Spiritual axes

You are quite likely to feel, 'Well it all depends . . .' or, 'Both are important to me.' Of course. We probably all need both ends of each axis and respond to each end at different times and in different ways. Nevertheless there is probably an instinctive preference in all of us, just as we instinctively pick up a pen with one hand or the other. It is that kind of preference this diagram asks for.

When the points on all the axes have been marked, join up the points with a pen-line drawn clockwise round the circle, like a 'join the dots' picture. You will end up with a shape, a blob!

This shape represents visually the contours of your own spirituality. There are three things to notice:

❊ **The first thing** to note is that this shape is utterly unique. No one else doing this exercise would come up with the same shape. Your relationship with God is like that – utterly unique. God loves, affirms and values the person you are, unconditionally.

❊ **The second thing** to notice is any parts of the shape which surprise you. Did you realize that you valued silence so much? Did you think that you were more keen on innovation in worship than this suggests? Is it annoying to be so moderate in everything?! What does the configuration say to you about yourself and your relationship with God?

* **The third thing** to ask yourself is – what would you like to change? What would you like to explore? There may not be anything in particular; you may be very comfortable with how you are. However, you may hear the Spirit's nudging to experiment in some new way – with symbols when you pray, for example. And if so, what will you do next to help bring that about?

The figure is a very impressionistic tool. It does not aim for any kind of exact science. Nevertheless it may offer a different and valuable way of understanding where you are at the moment in prayer and worship, and a way of reflecting upon the implications.

Moving on in study

One of the joys of ignorance is that there is so much left to learn! In the things of God there is an infinity of things to learn, but when we embark seriously on the Christian journey we are likely to have a hunger to find out more. Not all of us are readers or take to the disciplines of study, but it is nonetheless true that there has been an explosion of interest in studying the Bible, Christian belief, mission, ethical issues, practical ministry, relating to people of other faiths, and so on. There are at least four levels on which this continued thought and study can go on.

1 **Reading.** 'Of the writing of books there is no end.' Nor of the reading of them. Many people read the Christian books they are lent or which are recommended to them. Others wander round a Christian bookshop from time to time and see what interests them. Yet others might ask the minister for a book on so-and-so, and the really keen ones will ask for a reading course and the opportunity to discuss the books with the minister afterwards. In the Further Reading section following there is a range of suggested books which might be helpful. Do remember, however, these are only one person's suggestions from a huge range of possibilities, and that new – and maybe better – books are coming out all the time.

2 **Small groups.** Home groups and small groups of all kinds are ideal environments in which to learn, provided the material is right and the leaders know both how to use it and also how to get the most out of

a group. There is a huge range of resources available today, with the best way to find out being to write and ask for brochures on current courses from, for example:

✻ CPAS Sales, Athena Drive, Tachbrook Park, Warwick CV34 6NG (tel. 01926 334242).

✻ Bible Society, Stonehill Green, Westlea, Swindon SN5 7DG (tel. 01793 418100).

3 **Local courses.** Study courses are going on in churches all the time in most localities. Apart from study in home groups there will quite likely be day conferences, study days, local adult Christian education courses and more. Details usually appear in church magazines, Sunday bulletins and noticeboards. It is often the case in addition that there is a structured lay education and training course running at a central venue. In the Anglican church there is very often a Diocesan Certificate or equivalent with a flexible modular form, and those living near to a theological college may be able to drop into courses as an occasional student, without getting caught in the web of assessment.

4 **Distance learning and other assessed courses.** As educational provision has become more flexible and modular many different institutions have branched out into distance learning, whereby students undertake individual courses or even complete degree programmes through material sent out and marked by correspondence, together with occasional tutorial groups or residential periods. Students can progress at their own speed and work in their own time, and draw on local resources of people and libraries as appropriate. Amongst the more successful extension programmes are these:

✻ St John's Extension Studies, Chilwell Lane, Bramcote, Nottingham NG9 3DS.

✻ The Open Theological College, PO Box 220, The Park Campus, The Park, Cheltenham GL50 2QF.

✻ Oak Hill Open Learning Centre, Chase Side, Southgate, London N14 4PS.

It is also possible to embark on theological courses at certificate, diploma and degree level with theological colleges and university departments. All you need is minimum qualifications, proximity to the institution, and money for the fees!

Vocation

Vocation is really about 'hearing God's call'. When we have become caught up in the Christian life it often happens that people feel called to some form of Christian service. The danger is that some people will too easily interpret that call as one to be ordained because ordination seems to be the 'best' kind of call, and they want to give their best to God. We need to start a little further back.

It might help to distinguish between **three types of call:**

✱ **The call to be fully ourselves.** This is our first invitation from God. He wants us to be fully alive and fully ourselves, living up to our potential, firing on all cylinders. 'I have come that people may have life and have it abundantly,' said Jesus (John 10.10). We need to listen to the quiet but persistent inner voice that reminds us of our deepest nature, and to recognize the experiences and longings that excite our spirits. These are glimpses of our true self. The wise old rabbi Zusya said, 'When I get to heaven they will not ask me "Why were you not Moses?" They will ask me, "Why were you not Zusya?" '

✱ **The call to live the life of the baptized.** All Christians are called by God to live out their baptism; in other words, to live out the gospel in their own context. This is a call to be a Christian 'in the world' in the first place, not in the church. God's call is to be the salt which gives taste to a needy culture, and if his plan is to transform society it is no use the salt all staying together in the safety of the salt cellar. We need to be followers of Christ in the office, boardroom, kitchen, pub, and classroom. The test of our discipleship is not how comfortable we are in our church activities but how thoroughly we try to live out gospel values in the rest of our lives. Perhaps we ought to stick out like a healthy thumb! We may also, of course, be called to a particular ministry in the local church, and here too the range of roles and tasks is huge: to work with children, lead prayers in church, make the coffee, lead a study group, develop overseas links, visit the housebound, help with a homelessness project, be a welcomer on Sundays, and so on.

✱ **The call to accredited ministry.** This takes place when the wider church recognizes our gifts and, after appropriate preparation, asks us to exercise those gifts in its name. Accredited ministry comes in many forms:

- lay preacher or reader

- pastoral assistant

- Church Army evangelist

- mission partner working abroad

- ordained priest or minister – sometimes paid, sometimes unpaid, sometimes with authority only for a localized ministry.

When we embark on this particular journey the stakes are high and we need to be careful not to assume too much too soon. Most of all, we must not confuse a call to go deeper in our faith and witness with a call to ordination.

Responding to the call to accredited ministry

Let us assume, however, that you feel a 'divine restlessness' and believe it could be a call to some form of recognized public ministry. There are a number of things to be clear about, for example:

✻ A vocation of this sort will have to be both experienced within yourself and also recognized by the wider church. One without the other will not do.

✻ You will have to submit your sense of calling to some rigorous and searching process of discernment. When you are exercising a role as a public representative Christian the Church cannot afford to make too many mistakes in whom it chooses.

Here are some of the things that the Church, in whatever way it operates in different denominations, will want to be looking at. The following list applies particularly to full-time accredited ministries.

✻ **Ministry.** Do you understand what this particular form of ministry is all about and why it is exercised as it is in your church?

✻ **Vocation.** Can you speak coherently, realistically and with humility about your sense of vocation?

✻ **Spirituality.** Do you have a framework of personal and corporate prayer and worship which is still growing and is not exclusive?

✻ **Faith.** Can you demonstrate a personal commitment to Jesus Christ, and do you have an understanding of the faith, such that you can share it intelligently?

✳ **Educational potential.** Will you be able to cope with a rigorous course of theological study, and to be challenged by it without becoming defensive?

✳ **Character.** Have you the maturity, stability and flexibility needed in the demanding conditions of today's church? Integrity is crucial.

✳ **Relationships.** Have you sufficient self-awareness to develop open, healthy relationships both professionally and personally when engaged in ministry?

✳ **Leadership.** Do you have the ability to be a leader, earning the respect of others, and are you committed to working collaboratively rather than as a 'one-man band'?

There is a vast amount more to be said in this area of discerning a call to public representative ministry. Many people offer themselves for accredited ministry and are disappointed when they are not recommended for training by the wider church. The crucial thing is to realize that it is not a question of 'passing or failing'. It is a matter of finding what is the call of God for *you*, at *this* time, and the range of ministries, lay and ordained, is vast. Do not let your own ideas harden up. Keep them flexible and prayer-full.

The first step, however hard or far-fetched the idea of public ministry seems, is to go and talk to your own priest or minister. That's when the fun starts! But remember the wonderful words of Paul at the end of 1 Thessalonians: 'May God himself, the God of peace, make you holy in every part, and keep you sound in spirit, soul and body, without fault when our Lord Jesus Christ comes. He who calls you is to be trusted; he will do it.'

7　References and further reading

This is a very difficult section to put together, partly because of the huge range of available books, and partly because the journey each one of us makes is so unique. Moreover, books go out of print and new ones are always coming into the shops. What follows therefore is a resource list for reference and further reading, which has no more authority than the author's personal recommendation. It assumes a certain degree of serious-ness in following up the issues and subjects. If you talk to others you will get different suggestions, and if you wander around a Christian bookshop other books will take your eye. That's fine!

References

Thomas à Kempis, *The Imitation of Christ*, tr. Leo Sherley-Price, Penguin, 1952.

David Adam, *The Cry of the Deer*, Triangle, 1987.

Augustine, *Confessions*, tr. Henry Chadwick, Oxford University Press, 1991.

The Bible Speaks Today, Inter-Varsity Press.

The Cloud of Unknowing, ed. James Walsh sj, 'Classics of Western Spirituality' Series, Paulist Press, 1981.

Celebrating Common Prayer, Mowbray, 1992.

Anthony de Mello, *The Song of the Bird*, Doubleday Image, 1984.

Gregory Dix, *The Shape of the Liturgy*, Dacre Press, 1945.

Ruth Etchells, *Just As I Am*, Triangle, 1994.

Richard Higginson, *Mind the Gap*, Church Pastoral Aid Society, 1997.
E. Herman, *Creative Prayer*, Paraclete Press, USA, 1998.

Julian of Norwich, *Revelations of Divine Love*, tr. Clifton Wolters, Penguin, 1966.

Thomas Kelly, *A Testament of Devotion*, HarperCollins, 1992.

Henri Nouwen, *The Genesee Diary*, Darton, Longman & Todd, 1995.

John Pritchard, *The Intercessions Handbook*, SPCK, 1997.

Brother Roger, *His Love Is a Fire*, Geoffrey Chapman/Mowbray, 1990.

Believing

C. S. Lewis, *Mere Christianity*, Collins, 1952/1997. A classic presentation of the reasonableness of faith and its implications.

George Carey, *Letters to the Future*, Kingsway, 1998. A clear account of essential Christian beliefs by the Archbishop of Canterbury.

David Brown, *Invitation to Theology*, Blackwell, 1989. An introduction to the key methods used in studying theology.

Alister McGrath, *Christian Theology: An Introduction* (2nd edn), Blackwell, 1996. A first-class, readable and comprehensive guide for serious study.

John V. Taylor, *The Christ-like God*, SCM Press, 1992. A demanding but exciting entry into one area of theology.

Praying

Stephen Cottrell, *Praying through Life*, National Society/Church House Publishing, 1998. An accessible and practical book on relating prayer to all of life.

Paul Wallis, *Rough Ways in Prayer*, Triangle, 1991. An encouraging and readable book, useful when prayer has become a struggle.

Joyce Huggett, *Open to God*, Hodder & Stoughton, 1989. A much-used book opening up traditional methods of meditation in fresh ways.

David Adam, *Tides and Seasons*, Triangle, 1989. One of Adam's excellent series of books drawing on the Celtic tradition of prayer.

Anthony de Mello, *Sadhana: A Way to God*, Doubleday/Image, 1984. Christian exercises in meditation and silence using both Western and Eastern forms.

Gerard Hughes, *God of Surprises*, Darton, Longman & Todd, 1985. A classic bestseller on the spiritual journey and the use of imaginative prayer.

M. Goldsmith and M. Wharton, *Knowing Me, Knowing You*, SPCK, 1993. An exploration of the relationship of prayer to personality type, using insights from Myers-Briggs.

Ruth Fowke, *Personality and Prayer*, Eagle, 1997. A clear description of some of the issues in this area, and their implications for prayer.

Henri Nouwen has written many books which have been greatly valued by those taking the spiritual path seriously. So too Thomas Merton and Carlo Caretto on the 'desert tradition' of meditation and silent prayer. And then there are all the classics of previous centuries . . . !

Bible study

Terence Copley, *The Bible: The Story of the Book*, Bible Society, 1990. An attractive set of answers to lots of the basic questions we want to ask.

John Barton, *What is the Bible?* SPCK, 1997. One of the best starters on what the Bible is and what it means.

Stephen Barton, *Invitation to the Bible*, SPCK, 1997. A brief but thoughtful introduction to basic issues of modern biblical study.

The Lion Handbook to the Bible, Lion Publishing, 1999. Bright, readable, new edition of the comprehensive guide which has sold in millions.

John Bowker (ed.), *The Complete Bible Handbook*, Dorling Kindersley, 1998. Illustrated, colourful, accessible, up-to-date, huge coverage.

Raymond E. Brown, *An Introduction to the New Testament*, Doubleday, 1997. The best, big, one-volume introduction, helpful to novices and scholars alike.

Peter Gomes, *The Good Book*, Avon, 1998. A serious, thoughtful and witty exploration of the complex issues raised by scripture. Passionate and sometimes provocative.

Gerd Theissen, *The Shadow of the Galilean*, SCM Press, 1986. A wonderful narrative approach to the life of Jesus, using the best modern scholarship in an imaginative form.

Elizabeth Varley, *Catching Fire*, Bible Society, 1993. Imaginative ways of handling the Bible in church education programmes.

Hans-Ruedi Weber, *Experiments with Bible Study*, WCC, 1989. More advanced, participative encounters with the Bible.

Belonging to the church

Robert Warren, *Being Human, Being Church*, Marshall Pickering, 1995. A book which locates spirituality as the heartbeat of a church's life, and explores how this can empower congregations to be missionary in outlook and style.

Ruth Etchells, *Set My People Free*, Fount, 1995. A lay challenge to the churches to be more engaged with the world around them.

Richard Holloway, *Dancing on the Edge*, Fount, 1997. A compassionate, honest and sometimes controversial book for those prepared for a challenging, searching faith.

John McManners (ed.), *The Oxford History of Christianity*, Oxford University Press, 1992. An authoritative and detailed guide to the Christian centuries.

Ian Bunting (ed.), *Celebrating the Anglican Way*, Hodder & Stoughton, 1996. Comprehensive and readable introduction to Anglicanism.

Christian living

Nicky Gumbel, *Questions of Life*, Kingsway, 1995. A practical introduction to the Christian faith and its implications for belief and practice.

David Atkinson, *Pastoral Ethics in Practice*, Monarch, 1989. Brings biblical wisdom to bear on difficult ethical issues.

Nigel Biggar, *Good Life*, SPCK, 1997. An intelligent and thought-provoking book on what we value and why.

Robert Warren, *Living Well*, Fount, 1998. Applies the Beatitudes to the complex realities of Christian living today.

Philip Yancey, *What's So Amazing About Grace?* HarperCollins, 1997. A passionate and compelling account of the centrality of grace for Christians.

Vocation

Francis Dewar, *Called or Collared?* SPCK, 1991. A book which helps to distinguish different forms of vocation from each other.

Michael Ramsey, *The Christian Priest Today*, SPCK, revised edn 1985. The classic and deceptively simple book on Anglican ministry, still unsurpassed.

Michael Green, *Freed to Serve*, Hodder & Stoughton, 1983. A biblical study of what is involved in ordained ministry.

Robin Greenwood, *Transforming Priesthood*, SPCK, 1994. A searching and stretching contemporary account of Anglican priesthood.

George Guiver (ed.), *The Fire and the Clay*, SPCK, 1993. Reflections on what is meant by priesthood and what sort of priests the church needs.

And to feed the imagination

Mary Batchelor (comp.), *The Lion Christian Poetry Collection*, Lion, 1985. A feast of poetry from across the centuries.

Trevor Dennis, *Speaking of God*, Triangle, 1993; *Imagining God*, SPCK, 1997. Delightful collections of imaginative stories on biblical and Christian themes.